CNAC

老城市
OLD CITY

OLD SHANGHAI

A Lost Age

Text by Wu Liang

Text by: Wu Liang
Photos by: China No.2 Historical Archive
Shanghai Library
Translated by: Wang Mingjie
English text edited by: Foster Stockwell
Chinese text edited by: Wang Wentong

First edition 2001

Old Shanghai
— A Lost Age

ISBN7-119-02845-6

Published by Foreign Languages Press
24 Baiwanzhuang Road, Beijing 100037, China
Home Page: http://www.flp.com.cn
E-mail Addresses: info@flp.com.cn
sales@flp.com.cn
Printed in the People's Republic of China

Foreward

Despite many years living in a city, a person probably still has a relatively limited knowledge of it because of the limited nature of what one can see, experience, and hear over a whole lifetime.

We are residents of Shanghai, yet we often feel as though we are but travelers passing through this city. Whenever we enter a hotel to stay overnight, we first locate a local map, leaf through recent newspapers, look for the telephone numbers of a few friends, and then gradually get to know the surroundings: supermarkets, restaurants, bookstores, cinemas, etc. Shanghai is much too deep to fathom. It reveals its glamour to us from time to time. Although we find ourselves at home in this city, we are still outsiders. This is because we are so often surprised by seeing something new, something just discovered, even though we may be used to seeing the unexpected and dramatic. Surprise after surprise shows us that we are still outsiders.

It was that way with me. When faced with a pile of photos of old Shanghai, I was astonished, as you might be, even though there were a few that I had already seen. That was my first impression. Surprise stems from innocence. Surprise overthrows what I have already learned. What I am after is not knowledge but "surprise." It convinces me that I am but an outsider. Therefore, what I do is to view the pictures, to look on. Apart from this, there is nothing else I can do. One must plunge into life in order to experience life. But what fascinates me in books of photos is what happens to our own imagination.

Just like life, photos have no particular order, no content, no superiority or inferiority. Our reaction needs to be spontaneous, scrupulous and from instinct. Naturally, knowledge comes in good time, telling us what this picture is about, when it was taken, where it is, who is in the photo, what is there, and how to judge its contents, as well as which one to pick. Okay, let's say spontaneity and knowledge coexist. Knowledge serves as a tourist map that reminds us to catch the key points so as to avoid detours. It stresses effect. Spontaneity resembles a leisurely walk, which suits an outsider who may barge in or wander around. In these photos, let's give wings to our imagination; let's get lost or feel dizzy. There is always time to fish out the map to check where we are. There is no need to fear that you may not be able to find your way home.

One gets dual happiness from both a review and a trance in the lost age.

Wu Liang

August 1998, Shanghai

CONTENTS

Chapter 1 Review and Trance

(3) Incoherent Photos of An Old City
Photos Are the Warehouse that Stores All
(9) Stories in Detail
(17) A City Is But A Sand Table

A Bird's-eye View of Shanghai (23)
Old Fashions (25)
Common Objects and Photography (27)

(31) Stagnancy and Slowness
(35) Enthusiasm for New Fashions
(41) Photos Last Longer Than Reality

Chapter 2 Shadow Play of the Past

Portraits (49)
Daydreaming Among Photos (55)
Reeling Mill Women Workers on A Barrow (59)
Traces of Renowned Figures (63)

Wedding Ceremony in Western Style (65)
A Woman Getting on A Tram (71)
Rouged Women Ballad Singers at A Radio Station (77)

(81) Soundlessness
(85) Full of People
(87) Expression

Outsiders (89)
Hungry People (93)
Gambling (95)
Sellers of Little Stalls (99)

(103) Plump Women
(107) Four Dancers
(111) Mahjong
(115) A Gathering: Looking on Just for Fun

Chapter 3 Photos Are Traces of the Past

(121) Have and Have Not
(129) The Second Hometown
(133) Unknown Photographers

Many Buildings Are Like This (135)
Sasson Mansion and A Jazz Troupe Composed of Elders (139)
Stage Sets (143)
Interiors of Dwellings (147)
Mysterious Villas (151)

(155) Old Streets in Pictures
(161) Pharmacy and Soy Sauce Shop
(165) Silver Taxi Service

Public Telephone Booths (171)
Sheng Xuanhuai's Abacus (177)
Industry of Newspapers (179)

Chapter 4 A City with Human Temperature

(185) Famous Old Brands
(189) Strangers
(191) Lyceum Theater
(193) A Large Stage
(195) Churches

Paper-made Archway: An Old Theater (199)
Pawnshop (203)
Coffee Shops on the Map (205)
Inciting Cinemas (207)

(209) To Suit the Contemporary Times
(211) Out-of-Date Annotations
(217) Inconsistency

Progress, Fashion (221)
Demolition (223)
Flooded Streets (225)

Chapter 5 Through the Door of Impression

(231) Photography, Revolution and Documents
(233) A Repeatedly Used Photo
(237) Public Resistance
(239) "Another Page of Life Has Been Turned"

Chapter 1
Review and Trance

當

Incoherent Photos of An Old City

The Bund in 1850 (oil). From 1845 to 1849, Britain, the United States and France respectively established their concessions outside the northern entrance of the city.

Here was a pile of old photos, which had nothing to do with me. They had been put on my desk because they needed to be placed into albums. They all seemed to have origins (they were identified to have come from Shanghai by the architectural signs depicted, by the decorative objects on the clothing, and by scribbles on the blank parts of photos), but they were all independent, strange to one another, incoherent. A number of them bore no signs of time and location, which made them rather difficult to identify.

The span of time during which those photos were taken was probably one hundred years. I have neither love nor hatred for the city. What I do have is the ability to be held spellbound and to keep my distance. Having lived a long time in one city, I feel as if I have lived in all cities. "City" is an abstract word. It cannot

Longhua Temple, built in the period of the Five Dynasty Period (c. 907-930), was a famous ancient temple in the Yangtze Valley.

A barber's stall by a river (1932).

A Qing-dynasty court trial (1899).

be represented by any one particular city. Now I am going to plunge my hands into this pile of photos and stir them up as if I were playing with sand, mixing them up because, after all, they are all images of one city.

These photos are disconnected, illogical between themselves. There is no line which may link them together. Each photo tells its own story but without beginning nor end. Just as the theme of a photo is beginning to be discovered, it turns vague as soon as it is put beside another photo. Nothing fixed. Before you could pinpoint a theme of interest, it is gone with the wind. It is only a hovering fantasy without a centre. Before the image is fully coloured, it fades away instantly. Poetic language is unable to replace a photo which tells its longing, its own background without words. Behind that background is a moment of history. It is like a spectre trying to climb up from paper and declares: I am just like this. This is truly me. Please don't add anything else. You may take me as materials for nostalgia, because I am unable to repute it. Please look at me. Remember my image of the past. For this I would be most satisfied.

The past events in an old city will have long ago lost their vitality. No one cares to mention them anymore. But when they have made an impression on film, those magic films, they may become alive many years later. Old photos are as fresh to me as they might be in some dream that I have awakened from after a long hibernation. Even a dilapidated structure depicted in a photo will, when bathed in sunshine, become as bright as something brand new.

Longhua Pagoda (1874).

The temple of the town god was a place for residents to offer sacrifices to the god who was the protector of the town. The Temple of the Town God in Shanghai was first built in the early 15th century. By the 18th century, it had already become a recreational center for the town. This photo was taken in the 1920's.

In 1843, the Qing Court was forced by foreign powers to make Shanghai a port open to foreign trade. Foreign colonialists occupied the western bank of the Huangpu River and there built commercial blocks, banks, consulates, etc., which extended for 1.5 kilometers. It was then named "Waitan" or the Bund. The photo shows the Bund of 1853.

On 16 July 1901, Prince Zai Feng of the Qing Court (third from left on the gangway) arrived in Shanghai by way of the S. S. An Ping.

Nanjing Road in 1870. It was the eastern part of the present-day Nanjing Road and Fujian Road. In the late 1920's, Nanjing Road was the most prosperous business center in the Far East.

In 1850, a foreign company known as Lin Rui by force occupied a large stretch of land at the corner between present-day Nanjing Road and Henan Road (then known as the Five Sages Temple) and turned it into a garden that was named the Garden Lane. Later it was called the Great Street. In 1865, it was renamed Nanjing Road.

Photos Are the Warehouse that Stores All Stories in Detail

As we walk in a street, scenes seem to flow past on both sides. Normally, one might not pay close attention to them. They just brush past and rarely attract our attention. Sometimes, when I am looking for a particular store, I ignore looking for its number, an interesting advertising sign, or a familiar face. Even when I am in good mood and have plenty of time, looking left and right as I walk along like a tourist, I will still miss a lot of things. There are too many to notice. But each of those things has its origin, its own detailed story.

Human eyes are not camera lenses. They often miss things. They omit lots of useless details, unless these are part of what has been expected, what is exciting, and what should be focused on for knowledge. When we return home after a walk on a

Nanjing Road (1898).

Nanjing Road (1905).

A land demarcation marker in Shanghai.

street, we find it difficult to describe what we saw just an hour ago, unless it was an accident or some extraordinary event. A street can be a kaleidoscope in our minds with a myriad of colored objects churning around. How many pieces catch our attention? Since most are irrelevant to us, we simply ignore them because our

A bank on Nanjing Road.

energy is limited and we don't want to be too nosy. So our quick steps just leave them behind and they never leave a deep impression on our minds. There is no

Stores on Nanjing Road in the late Qing dynasty.

room for such items in the warehouse of our memories.

We may even be surprised by what we see in a photo of a street. Only the impartial camera is able to take in every detail in a scene. This provides us with a good opportunity to have a look at all aspects of the street. The objects remain unmoved, and do not hide themselves because of our prejudice. Each detail has its place in the frame of a limited square.

These photos, taken some fifty to a hundred years ago, may be quite familiar to us. However, they are worth another look. Five-colored flags used along streets after the 1911 Revolution, rickshaws, bicycles, an advertisement for Beauty Cigarettes, hydrants, elec-

The Sincere Company on Nanjing Road.

trical poles, the Nanyang Pharmacy, the Ouyang Dentist, Dr. Zhou Jipu, double-decker trams, Shouerkang, a candle and incense shop, a young couple, sunshine, shadows.... The kaleidoscope of the street was thus photographed, giving us views that are more reliable than any eyes. All the details of a street have been taken in by an impartial camera, though the image lacks profundity. But as an illustration of modern history, it should be enough to satisfy later generations.

The Town Hall on Nanjing Road.

Advertisements and neon lights could be seen everywhere along Nanjing Road. This photo was taken in the 1920's.

Five-colored flags fluttered in the wind after the success of the Shanghai Uprising in 1911.

A bird's-eye view of Nanjing Road. The building in the center was the Da Sun Company (present-day No. 1 Department Store of Shanghai).

A renowned teahouse named the Green Lotus Pavilion. It later became a store.

The New Northern Gate (1860).

A City Is But A Sand Table

I promised to write a book entitled *Old Shanghai - A Lost Age* for a publishing house. Though the title was already decided upon, I did not start the project immediately.

I knew this city well for I had been to almost all its streets and alleys. However, I was not sure how to write about it. I was like a child entering a Children's Playground with no idea as to what toy to play with first. All the publishing house provided was the title. Where should I start? Sometimes, when I sauntered in a street of this city, I could not help thinking: Was it enough to learn about a city just by looking at a pile of old photos? It would not help much to browse among books and in the archives. Should I, I wondered, start with a barber's shop, a restaurant, a wine shop sign or a street lamp?

The deadline for providing the manuscript was fast approaching, but I still whiled away my time in walking the streets, my mind rather empty. Around ten o'clock one day, as I sat sipping coffee under an awning by the street, I lifted my head and looked at the building across the Street. A sunbeam illuminated one window on its top floor, casting a blue shadow that extended to the foot of the structure. I decided to

The building of the Four-Bank Deposit Council, an institution established jointly by four banks, namely, the Salt Industry, Jincheng, Zhongnan and Continental.

A Shanghai woman in the 1920's.

proceed to the top floor of that building.

About ten minutes later, I poked my head out of the window to look down. I could not see the chair I had just been sitting on. Even the red awning was somewhat blurred. I looked forward and the city seemed to have disappeared. What was left was a model, a large sand table, to be precise. The kind of sand table used by generals in war briefing rooms. All of the details no longer existed. Only some landmark buildings remained.

Down there, traffic was heavy. Stores, advertisements, coffee tables, and faces of different kinds had all disappeared. What I could see was a large sand table. I looked again. The sun was dazzling. So there was the sun over the city, which I had not noticed before.

Renji, a foreign-invested Company (1908).

S.M.C. Administration Building, built in 1913, stood at the junction of Fuzhou and Jiangxi Roads.

An aerial view of the center of Shanghai (1937).

An aerial view of Xujiahui (1930's).

Sichuan Road Bridge over Suzhou Creek.

With foreign trade in the concessions along the Bund and internal trade at Shiliupu, Shanghai entered the industrial age and the world economic system. Trading of all kinds became brisk. Its good environment for investment made it one of the most important cities in China and even in the Far East.

A Bird's-eye View of Shanghai

As one's eyes took in a bird's-eye view, Shanghai, even in those earlier times, would have resembled an artistic mosaic. It would have rolled out ceaselessly towards horizon. It was a world made of small pieces, one after another. Each piece had its own unique feature. Diversified tastes, different life styles were all piled up together, which resulted in tolerance, surprises, distaste, dizziness, excitement and ambition.

By this, we may be able to imagine another type of city, a model for all cities. In fact, textual study may not hold reign in all fields. As long as we do not venture into the academic world, we can try our imaginations. What I saw was a city of the past. Now I live in this city which is no longer the one I see in the photos.

The photo shows the building of North China Daily News. On the left stood the statue of the Municipal Chief Officer of Taxation of the time.

A post office at the North Railway Station in Shanghai (1947).

Old Fashions

Whenever some people see a few curios, their blood begins to boil. Even old photos make their hearts beat faster. A sepia portrait of a girl with an ordinary face may ignite their enthusiasm. A dilapidated microphone that can no longer produce any pleasant sounds is stubbornly believed to reproduce melodious music. Things like a Western suit that does not look quite right and the portrait of a lady with a tasteless perm are still highly praised. This is of course not appropriate. But people like to think that way. Old fashions have always been an enemy of modernity. The term "old fashions" here refers to those things that went out of date just a few years ago. As for things from dozens of years or even a century ago, these have become fashionable once more.

At midnight on 28 January 1932, Japanese troops suddenly attacked the Chinese army stationed in Zhabei in Shanghai. The photo shows Chinese people flooding into foreign concessions.

A bird's-eye view of the lower reach of the Wusong River in the 1930's.

Common Objects and Photography

Common objects provide endless resources for photographers. We are surrounded by miscellaneous objects and have no time to discover the poetry or tragedy contained in them. Photography provides a solution, for it is able to give us time to evaluate the objects. For a split second, a common object may show us something extraordinary. Of course, that may not happen until many years later. From an old photo, people of today may discover moments of poetry or tragedy.

The effects of photography often grow as time passes. A number of photos will help to broaden the vistas of a scene. One particular photograph may have recorded a good subject. However, just one cannot present a complete panoramic view of any place. It would not be enough to satisfy the reader who is eager to know more.

An ordinary object may become significant only

when it appears as the theme of a photo. The viewer will be moved by the photo of this object, but not by the object itself. The lusterless eyes of a hungry man in a photo will shock us and arouse our sympathy. But if you came across such a pair of eyes when walking in a Street, you might not be sympathetic. In this sense, photography is a lot more effective than human eyes. It is able to detect and catch something shocking, or something romantic or grievous. But this effect is actually the result of a viewer giving up his visual rights. The viewer yields his preemptive rights of sight to the object produced by a photographer. It is through

The chair designated for the chairman of the board of directors of the Municipal Council in the International Settlement.

A dock near Nanjing Road along the Bund.

Portrait of a woman from a well-off family (1920's).

photos, picture albums, news reports, and theme exhibitions that we learn about the world we live in.

A rickshaw and a bicycle (late Qing dynasty).

A banquet (late Qing dynasty).

Stagnancy and Slowness

A rickshaw of the late Qing dynasty.

It was many years before the ways of Western life were introduced into the city. Before that the long pigtails, robes, bound feet of women, grand ceremonies for weddings or funerals, officials in sedan-chairs could be seen everywhere. The opening of ports to trade and commercial and industrial development did not yet affect the lives of ordinary people much. Those at the top tended to be even more conservative.

The impression one gets from the old photos of Shanghai is stagnancy and slowness. The people are solidified. Their history, recorded by photography, is solidified too. The expression of those Chinese in the photos has remained on their faces for centuries. However, upheaval, revolution and revelry would be coming soon. Suffering promoted changes. People were involved in the new endeavors without realizing it. A new era was already at the threshold.

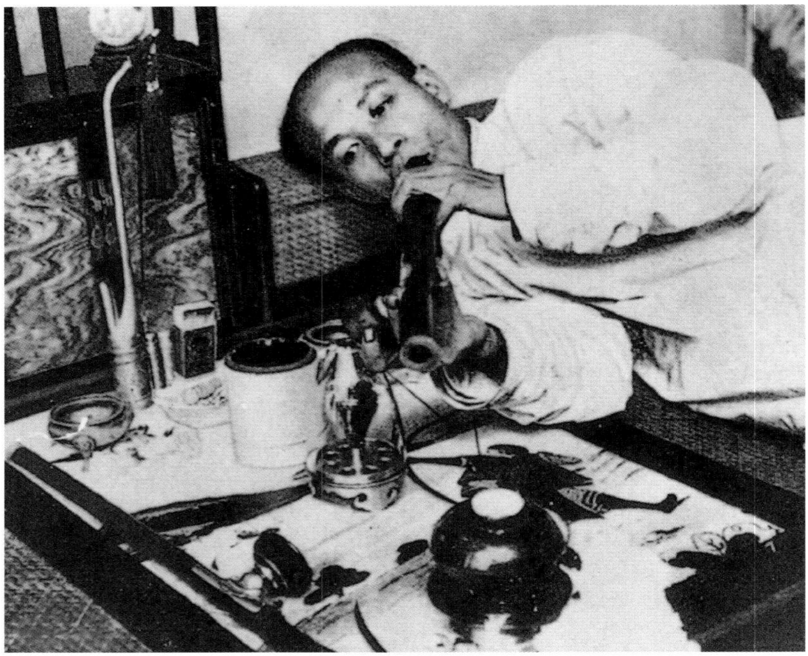

An opium addict.

The car of a British diplomat was burnt in a street (1906).

Bound feet. This backward practice gradually died out in the 1920's and 1930's.

Outside of a cathedral in Shihutang Village of Shanghai.

The three winners in a dog race in Canidrome in 1935.

Audience at a dog race in Canidrome.

A pageant for "Miss Shanghai."

Enthusiasm for New Fashions

The interesting part of a photo often lies with the fact that there is no theme, or perhaps the theme has been temporarily shelved.

If photography only sought to show something interesting, one would lose their aim when taking photos in a city. It would be a waste of film. Blindness and thoughtlessness would turn the camera into just a piece of machinery, with the photographer dashing like a cat about the city. It would be a totally senseless endeavor.

Among the big pile of photos, one of a beauty parlor caught my attention. Several women were leisurely looking at themselves in some large mirrors. Behind the busy attendants there was a door open to a street. Outside, the sunshine dazzled brightly and a few pedestrians passed by. The purpose of this photo

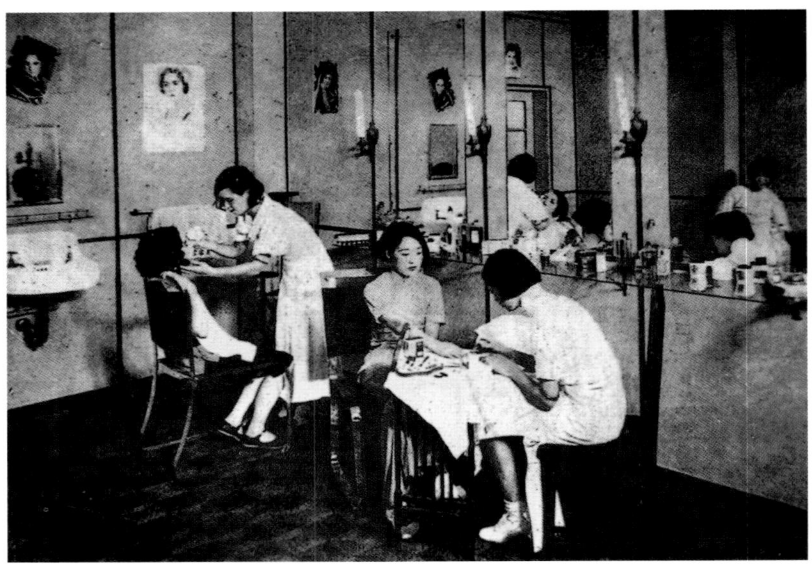

A high class beauty parlor for women from prestigious families, film stars and social butterflies.

was perhaps to record a scene of life and to reflect the rise of beauty parlors, a new trade in the city. At that time, such a scene was of no great significance. But today it is rather meaningful.

Life in a city is composed of almost everything in each and every corner and at all times. A pedestrian may glance at all this activity whether he is in a hurry or is just taking a stroll. He may become curious, enthusiastic or suspicious on the spot. But inevitably he

Passengers on a ferry boat.

A pedestrian (1930's).

would forget what he has seen. The lens of a camera will freeze an ordinary scene regardless of what is flowing by. Years later, someone may be fascinated by such a scene among the pile of photos, believing there was some profound truth in the decision to photograph it or even thinking that its message is eternal.

The Shanghai Office of the British Sunalliance Insurance Company.

The Sincere Company, the largest department store in Shanghai, taken in the 1920's.

A photo is symbolic of nothing. All it could provide is a little bit of interest. To look at a photo is a par to looking at the past which is lost for ever. Still such an act is significant. People of later generations fondle those photos with their eyes, just like those objects in the photos were once fondled by light (not necessarily sunlight).

A winter scene of Jingansi Road (present-day West Nanjing Road) taken in the 1920's.

The junction between Avenue Joffre and Shanzhong Road was a quiet place for living quarters.

The junction between Wusong Road and Haining Road, taken in 1920's.

Photos Last Longer Than Reality

One morning I happened to see a photo depicting the entrance to a bookstore on Fuzhou Road. It was not a clear picture, and it was produced in sepia tones. However, it had been made into a post card and was on the display counter in the store. There were also several other old photos of Shanghai. As reproductions for tourists, all of them looked brand new.

But I was fascinated by the one showing the entrance to the store. It had been taken in the 1930's. I was so surprised to see it that I simply gaped at the picture. So this was Huaihai Road of some 60 years ago! What amazed me was that there was no sign of activity or prosperity on the whole street. Tranquility was probably the best word to describe the scene. I seemed to be able to smell the fragrance of flowers.

The photo was probably taken in the early morning because the Wuchang Grocery, on the left side of the photo, was not yet open for business. There were few pedestrians. Except for a man in a light-colored robe walking along and a rickshaw boy wheeling his rickshaw along the street, most people were engulfed in shade. To the right stood the present-day department store for women, which used to be an apartment building. Further down the street, there was a patch of sky. At that time, the Yong Ye Building had not yet been built nor other large department stores, which were built only a few years before.

The photographer must have taken his position

Avenue Joffre (present-day Huaihai Road). In 1900, the western side of the French Concession was expanded to Lu Ban Road (present-day Chongqing Road). The next year, the four-kilometer-long Baochang Road (present-day Central Huaihai Road) was built. This road later became the second busiest street in Shanghai.

on the top floor of the Old Hu Kaiwen Brush Store. This structure was located on the southern side of Huaihai Road, close to the junction where Danshui

In 1914, Joffre, who had come to Shanghai as a military engineer, was appointed the general commander of the Eastern Route Army of France. He saved France by the victory of the Marne in World War I. The authorities of the French Concession changed the name of this street to Avenue Joffre in honor of him. The photo shows Avenue Joffre in late 1930's.

Road crossed it. Here the photographer was able to include the whole panoramic view in his camera lens.

A photo produced on a piece of paper is rather fragile and vulnerable to damage. Yet it is most durable. It is able to preserve a scene of reality for a very long time in this flat form. The object in the photo itself is actually in a state of instability. Therefore, a photo often lasts longer than reality. A photo is able to make me stare at it spellbound because some objects in it no longer exit. But its "signs" are still discernible. It also tells me that the location of space remains unchanged, but time forever slips away. All the objects in this street scene are quite amazing. This is particularly so because this is a street I have known since my childhood. Even today it often appears in my dreams.

This new style building known as Shi Ku Men was constructed in Baochang Road (present-day Central Huaihai Road) in early 20th century.

The Broadway Mansion.

請吸
高樓牌香煙
福利德香煙
穉英

Chapter 2
Shadow Play of the Past

An advertisement for a printing company.

Portraits

This is a portrait of a well-known prostitute during the late Qing dynasty (1644-1911). It had been locked in an archive box for years and was rediscovered at a time when nostalgia was in vogue. It has been included in some historical albums and has become known throughout the city. The woman in the picture, now familiar to many, looks shy and sexy. Her melancholy mood and degeneration, together with her pretty face, perished a century ago.

Historical records trace prostitution back to late Ming dynasty (1368-1644). In *Jottings After Ink*, the author said, "At the west end of the city there were a series of fancy houses in deep alleys." At that time this city had not yet become a paradise for foreigners. Later on, when Shanghai became an open port to for-

Prostitutes of the late Qing dynasty.

eign trade, many of the fancy houses moved into the foreign concessions. Prostitution became a brisk business. Most of those fancy houses were located in Fourth Street and Huileli Lane. It was not until 1949 when the People's Republic of China was founded that the business of prostitution was scrapped.

This photo shows a smart woman with misty eyes, tightly closed lips, and a fashionable hair-do and dress. We don't have to guess her identity since she was identified by some learned scholar as a "singsong girl." The caption has limited our imagination. The photo itself is innocent, for it cannot determine its own fate. Because photos can be circulated, seeking truth (photos for news) and textual research (old photos) are two important keys to be used in interpreting old pictures. So, in my view, when looking at (not glancing) such a portrait, it is better not to read the caption. A pretty face itself is visually pleasant. There is no need to have any description of it. No one knows exactly who Mona Lisa was. Her history is meaningless to viewers. What amazes us is her dreamy smile. This is because it is a famous oil painting, not a photograph to annotate history.

Calendar portrait of a Shanghai woman painted by Jin Meisheng.

Two prostitutes enjoy a ride on a "spaceship" (1913).

Fuzhou Road in the early 20th century.

Prostitutes of the early 20th century.

A photo taken during the late Qing dynasty in a studio of its early days.

Photo of the Bund taken in mid 1930's.

Daydreaming Among Photos

Since photography has come into being, time can be frozen or reversed.

To review a photo means to go back in time. This can be an immense consolation for human beings. Whenever and wherever an old photo is discovered, it revives lost loves and transports one to an earlier time.

To leaf through a stack of past photos is one of the best ways to while away one's time. Because a pleasant period in the past can be contained in a single photo, it is possible to thus relive one's life. And what we have today, such as sunshine, joy, a tranquil evening, or a party may also be reappeared in this way in the future.

A photo can be one of the best means for reminiscence. It can correct errors in detail, locations and people's names. It is a tracing of life.

To flash back in time is something like going back to a lost playground. It is a method for reliving reality. The very existence of a photo shows an existence of something past. It also means that each time you look at it, the life of something past extends. Since it is viewed time and again, it has become a kind of pioneer of such existence. It did happen once in the past. Because of this, it has reasons to be view by the people of today.

The figure in a photo has nothing to do with us. We live in a different time and in a different area of the country. However, the photo causes dreamy thoughts all the same. Dreamy thoughts are usually not copies or simple distortions of a past life. They stem from much more indirect experiences. For example, one can dream of a street fair at the entrance to a town of a hundred years ago. The vendors and customers are milling about. The sign streamers of a store are fluttering in the breeze. Such scenes often appear in our minds like the shadow plays we saw in childhood. A Christmas party of some sixty years ago, for example, well-dressed young women, music of waltz, waiters, brightly lit ballrooms, etc. often become one

This picture was taken in 1920's.

A show of performing stars (1934).

of my regular daydreams.

Without photography, our knowledge of earlier days would erode and disappear. Since the appearance of photos in this world, we have been able to return to a life that no longer exists.

The Wusong River taken between 1930's to 1940's.

Women workers for the Shanghai Silk Mill went to work on a barrow (1930's).

A barrow taken in early 20th century.

Reeling Mill Women Workers on A Barrow

To add a caption to a photo is something like having obtained authorization: either you have learned about the photo's origin, secrets, and background information or no one knows about the object in the photo. Professional monopoly provides power; others' ignorance serves as the basis for such power.

According to the record of the 1980's, "In Shanghai, industries of rubber, silk reeling, flour, enamel products, woolen fabrics, cotton yarns and cotton cloth have more or less grown." This sentence can be used for reference in what follows.

Economic prosperity does not mean that the life of the working class must always remain poor. The women workers in the photo were obviously well dressed. There was no sign that they were maltreated. Of course, such a supposition is dangerous. A photo found by chance may not contain universal truth. Only the statistics provided by sociologists can be authoritative.

A photo may convince our eyes, but it cannot be used as a conclusion. Very often, it is some interesting but insignificant discovery, observation, perusal or guess-work that may attract our attention.

These women workers look like students. Their postures do not appear to be those of workers at all. They are looking at someone outside of this photo, as if complaining, "You are late again!"

This barrow is waiting for someone. Perhaps it was time to take a holiday and the women had put on their white clothes and white socks, looking forward to a family reunion. Thoughts such as these are not strange. The long shadows cast on the ground indicate that it is in the gloaming of an evening. It is a time for relaxation, laziness and satisfaction.

Women workers of the Yangshupu Textile Factory are on their way to work.

An advertisement truck of the Xinfeng Silk Weaving and Printing Factory in a motor-vehicle parade for the Year of Women and Domestic Products.

Jardine Cotton Mill in Yangshupu.

Gathering to celebrate the completion of the municipal government building in 1933.

Funeral procession for Ruan Lingyu (1935).

Traces of Renowned Figures

Renowned figures are always targets for a camera lens. Such persons appear at evening parties, ribbon cutting ceremonies, charitable or donation activities, shaking hands, making speeches, traveling and visiting, etc. All these offer a kind of public show. Occasionally, without their knowing it, public figures are caught by cameras, which is known as "exposure."

Renowned figures seen on public occasions are quite careful about their appearances, which is indicated by their dress, decorations and smiles. No matter how true it might be, people invariably think they are making history, whereas the term "exposure" is probably closer to the truth even though the photographers might be charged with being shameless, making personal gain, or "creating a big stir for personal fame." Because of photography and the circulation of photos, renowned figures are topics for people's conversation, from which they obtain privilege and interests. At the same time, the renowned persons earn themselves rumors and slanders.

Picture at a wedding ceremony in the early 20th century.

Picture of a Western wedding ceremony held in the Shanghai Concession during the late Qing dynasty.

A picture of a wedding ceremony (early 20th century).

Wedding Ceremony in Western Style

Shanghai has long been a place that is highly influenced by Western styles and manners. This can be demonstrated by an insignificant photo of a wedding ceremony.

A bow tie, dark suit, white wedding dress, red roses, a pair of white gloves held in hand, all these items of apparel and decoration were both Western and local. It is an interesting phenomenon in China. People tried to improve their old practices but fell into new stereotypical patterns. The traditional wedding ceremony was easily cast away. Sedan chairs were replaced by cars decorated with flowers; kowtowing to Heaven and Earth were replaced by making pledges in churches; the lady in charge of a wedding ceremony was replaced by a Master of Ceremonies. A bride did not have to go through the process of hair-do making and cleansing of facial hair. She began to perm her hair by means of electricity or chemical fluids. The red cloth head square was a thing of past. She no longer had to show even the slightest shyness. Instead she would hold the bridegroom's arm in high spirits, and let the photogra-

A bride in a wedding dress (1930's).

phers take pictures of the couple surrounded by relatives and friends.

At a relatively formal wedding ceremony in Western style there were also the best man and bridesmaids, accompanied by a boy and a girl. All the men stood on the left side of the bridegroom; all the women stood on the right side of the bride. Children would stand at the front. They wore shorts and skirts and high white knee socks, looking like little angels. Everyone looked bright and charming, modest and polite.

"Westernization" in this old photo is part of the history of the city. It serves as a witness to its history. Western suits, gauze wedding dresses, and roses were so familiar to people that no one would ask where all this originated. The ceremonies had nothing to do with their origins, but were passed from one person to another. They ignited people's enthusiasm for life and gave people new opportunities for imagination.

There was no tradition that could remain forever in Shanghai. People in this city tended to imitate the

Many young couples were fond of having Western style wedding ceremonies.

A wedding ceremony held on a ferry-boat.

A collective wedding ceremony held in front of the auditorium of the Jiangwan government (1934).

The tenth collective wedding ceremony of the industrial and commercial circles organized by the Shanghai General Trade Union.

practices in some foreign countries, and they were not keen on preserving the customs of their forefathers. Therefore, wedding ceremonies, a Western custom, together with other aspects of Western culture and promoted by guns and warships, entered this land. This was indeed a strange phenomenon.

In a short period of half a century, all the traditions have been changed. Sedan chairs, *suona* trumpets, the red head square and red candles have all become stage sets or decorative objects for films of an oriental legendary nature. Another legend has now been exaggerated: Westernized Shanghai, the Paris of the East. Imitation has given the city an exotic atmosphere. It is still seeking for common ground with foreign countries. At the same time, it has a little more reason from history: Look, this is how our grandpa and grandma got married.

A tram used first by the Shanghai Tram Company (1914).

A Woman Getting on A Tram

This photo should be regarded as an "old photo" even though it was taken in the 1930's or 1940's. A woman is getting on a tram, a rolled up newspaper in her hand. She is wearing an improved *qi bao* (a close-fitting woman's dress with high neck and slit skirt), revealing part of her calf. We are unable to see what kind of shoes she is wearing. But we can clearly see that her hair is bobbed. I guess that she was hurrying back home and whiled away her time by reading the newspaper. There are not many passengers in the tram. Several people sit by the windows at the back of the tram, all wearing hats. The street is rather deserted except for a young man dressed like a worker on the docks, who is exiting the picture. He seems to be looking around. His cap indicates the fashion of the time and also reveals his occupation and social status. The street is rather wide. At that time, Shanghai did not have many streets like this one. Probably this was

A test run of a tram on a tramway in 1908.

present-day Nanjing Road, or Yangshupu Road, because at that time trams were already available in some parts of the city, as they were in the French and British concessions.

The woman getting on the tram would never have expected that some thirty years later a woman writer named Zhang Ailing would often take the tram and write about it in one of her stories. Of course, this author also wrote about balconies, sitting rooms, lifts in apartment buildings and bathrooms.

A tram stop on Nanjing Road.

The French Concession on the Bund (late 1920's).

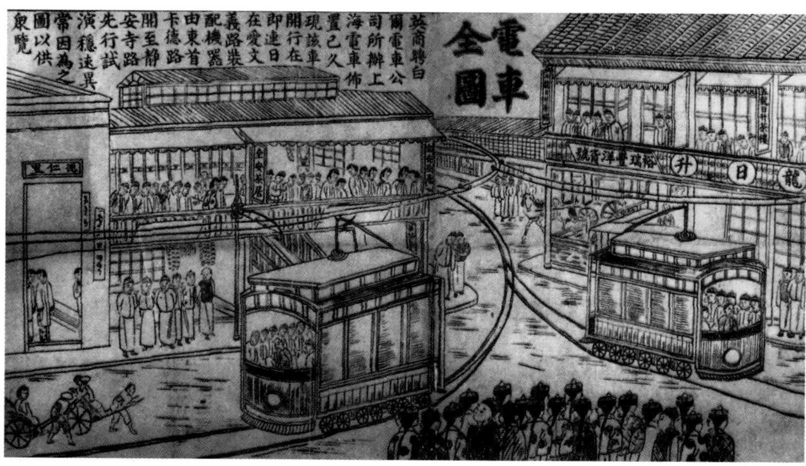

A poster advertising the tram built by a British company.

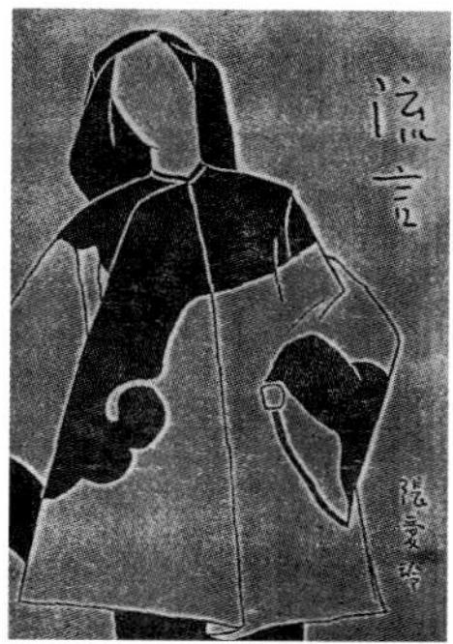

The first edition of *Gossip*, A collection of prose writings by Zhang Ailing.

Zhang Ailing was born in Shanghai in 1921. She graduated from St. Mary's Girls School of Shanghai. She published her first story *The Dream of A Genius* in a monthly magazine named *The West Wind* in 1939. In 1952, she went to Hong Kong and in 1955 went to the United States. Her main works are *The Golden Cangue*, *Love in Redland*, *Legend*, *Gossip*, etc.

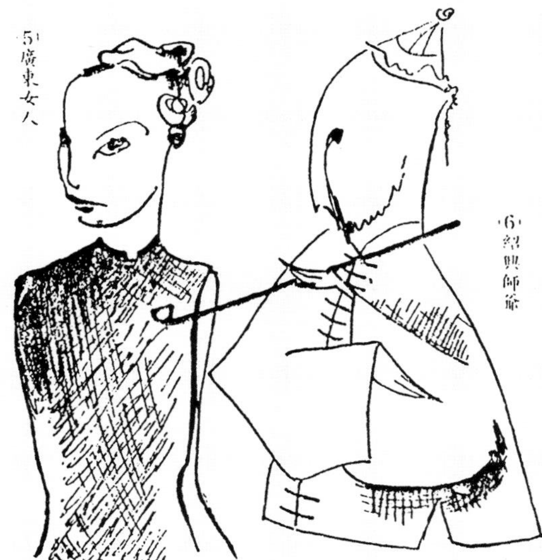

A sketch by Zhang Ailing

A calendar portrait painted by Hang Zhiying.

A night scene on Nanjing Road (mid-1930's).

Rouged Women Ballad Singers at A Radio Station

In the 30's and 40's of the 20th century, calendars printed with pictures of beauties dressed fashionably were quite popular in Shanghai. One quiet night, I came across such a calendar depicting two rouged ballad singers at a radio station. They looked lifelike and vivid, with charming smiles and fair arms set off by a pink background. I seemed to hear their soft singing coming from afar. Gradually, a page from the past seemed to have been turned and I sensed the bright life of commoners during a short-lived time of prosperity. In 1923, the Shanghai Radio began broadcasting programs. Renowned opera stars and their melodious tunes entered many households. It was a time of parties and merriment, a time for singsong girls and dancers. Laughter went together with tears. Moneybags,

A ballroom (1933).

The American-invested radio station began broadcasting on the night of 3 January 1923. This was the first broadcasing station in Shanghai.

employees, love affairs.... kept revolving like a merry-go-round in front of my eyes. Then there were *qi bao*, rickshaws, the pungent smell of coffee, clanking trams,

Both Chinese and foreign dancers enjoy dance music.

noises in a sitting room.

I woke up from the dream wondering how a picture on a calendar could send me into such a trance. After all, it was but a picture, not even a photo. I was unable to provide myself with historical details.

All the elements in the picture showed the fashion of that time and indicated the poor annotation of such fashion by the painter – a pattern of the Western way of life. However, this was another version of the New Year's pictures found in the countryside, at least as far as artistic technique

Operators (1936).

was concerned. Meticulous brushstrokes, rubbing, plus the newly learned perspective, yet the painting was unable to depict the truth of metropolitan life, although it might reveal the truth of what was being sought after.

Students performing Shakespeare's *The Merchant of Venice.*

Soundlessness

A girls school, reading Shakespeare, greeting teachers in English, a boarding school, spare-time drama society, all those created an atmosphere that was familiar yet strange. Western civilization, colonial cultural invasion, modern education could all be used to annotate those soundless photos. "History is a girl who can be decorated at will." This is a famous, yet old metaphor. It has brought about all kinds of historic views.

This photo shows some female students performing Shakespeare's *Twelfth Night*. Unfortunately the faces of the actors are not clear. Dresses with tightly fastened belts, hats, roughly painted sets, a poem on the gate, all indicate that it was but a game. Though soundless, I am quite certain that it must have been a

Charlie Chaplin, the great American comedian, visited Shanghai. The photo shows him meeting Ma Lianliang after seeing him perform in the Peking Opera *Famen Temple* at the Xinguang Theater.

holiday or a weekend night. The girls' parents and relatives must have been sitting and watching them act. They must have come from well-off families and their future was well arranged. They first studied in colleges like Saint John's and then went abroad to study.

All these imaginings are irrelevant. A photo itself is a subject. What is the predicate? The photo has a very brief caption: "Students of the McTyeir's School perform Shakespeare's *Twelfth Night*."

This is good enough to help us understand the photo. However, the predicate cannot be reined in. It is like a horse without rein and has galloped away. So,

Girl students of McTyeir's School performing Shakespeare's *Twelfth Night.*

urged by soundlessness, we have to imagine what is the predicate, to imagine an evening half a century ago, to imagine that the Shakespearean play was half way through in an auditorium of a girls school.

A temple fair at Jingan Temple (1930's).

A ten thousand ton freighter made by the Jiangnan Shipyard began to sail in 1918.

A national sport meet held on 10 October 1935 in Shanghai Central District Stadium (present-day Jiangwan Stadium).

Full of People

Shanghai at that time was already full of people. Crowded residential buildings deprived people of a space in which to take a leisurely walk. Except for those areas where some foreigners resided, the whole city could be described in one word: chaotic. It was noisy, squalid, disorderly, and crowded. Surely you may also call the people in the picture full of commotion, vital, prosperous, bustling with activity. It all depends on how you look at it.

A bank clerk.

A rickshaw boy.

Expression

One's facial expression often reveals his or her nationality, social status and occupation. A newspaper reporter with a hat, a waxen-faced rickshaw boy, a bored singsong girl.... They provide good references for film actors and actress in make-up.

Indeed, we may judge a person's nutrition, life tempo, consumption of physical energy, and even his family background, financial situation and prospective by looking at his face. As for his origin and fate, one has to guess. In the world of today, anything could be the case. But the differences between different social strata are not easily altered. They are written on each face. So with one glance, you may be able to tell to which class or which circle he or she belongs to without much thought.

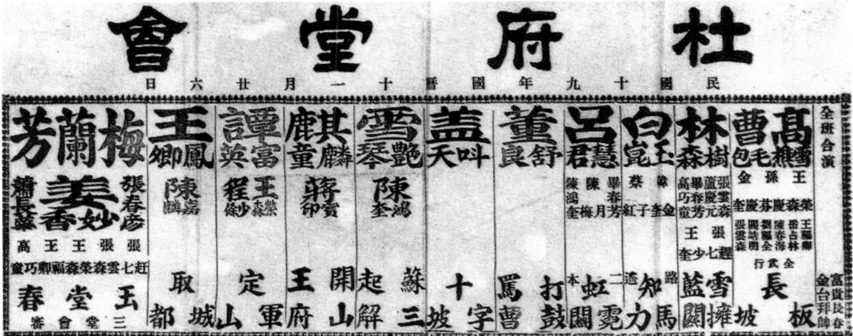

A program of Peking Opera Performances on the occasion of the completion of the Clan Hall of Du Yuesheng in 1931.

Picture of all the famous Peking opera performers of Beijing and Shanghai.

Du Yuesheng (1888-1951), together with Huang Jinrong and Zhang Xiaolin, was one of the three ring leaders of the Qing Bang Triad.

Outsiders

Renowned figures like Yu Jiaqing, Du Yuesheng, Huang Jinrong, and the like are much described in some biographical novels, newspaper articles, historical records, films, and serial TV dramas. But how many people have ever read or watched them? The designation of "renowned figure" can be a rather subtle phrase. It can be commendatory as well as derogatory. In the past, such persons were known as big shots, noted public figures, ringleaders, and chief gangsters.... They had complicated backgrounds, were men of the world, involved in all kinds of intriguing love affairs and hatreds, and they often appeared in all kinds of disguises.

Many legendary stories from Shanghai depict such renowned figures, or their shadows. In this metropolis

The race course in the late Qing dynasty. It was turned into the People's Square in 1954.

Famous triad leaders Du Yuesheng and Zhang Xiaolin.

Scene of celebration when Yu Qiaqing Road was so named in 1936. Nine years later, it was renamed Central Tibet Road.

right and wrong, prosperous and gloomy, pompous and conspicuous, internal strife, and collaboration always make people curious to find out who was behind all these things. In reality, those renowned figures have nothing to do with us. Their only connection is that they lived in Shanghai in the past and we live in the same city half a century later. Why are we interested in them? Because they were once famous. Good or bad, after a long period of time, we do not care any more. We are outsiders, spectators of history.

卦令如神

A little refugee in war time.

Hungry People

When I open my photo albums, I often feel delighted. But sometimes I have an indescribable fear. Our fellow countrymen, also living in a prosperous world, were unfortunate, exhausted, dull, hungry, ignorant and even waiting for death. Photos are photos. They can heal a wound but also touch a wound. This cannot be avoided or skirted.

Like all metropolises, Shanghai has always been propped up by millions of unknown workers. They are the backbone of society. It is important to understand this before going into other things.

The 28.7-hectare race course, first built in 1862, was the site for the later People's Park, People's Square and the Shanghai Library.

A gambling stand during the late Qing dynasty.

Gambling

Gambling usually brings to mind luck, speculation, daydreaming of getting rich, fraud, making profits by other people's toil, and adventure. Gambling at the bottom of society is usually connected with triads, crimes and evils. Playing tricks, magic ways, cheating, covering-up, instinct and probability, and trusting to luck are always the main elements of stories about gambling.

Gambling in cities in modern times is covered up by civilized procedures and well-knit organizations. Signs and numbers camouflage the setups and traps.

Tossing dice in a street is certainly different from putting a stake on a horse in a horse race, though both are gambling. The former is regarded as decadent or low, whereas the latter is refined and even of high class.

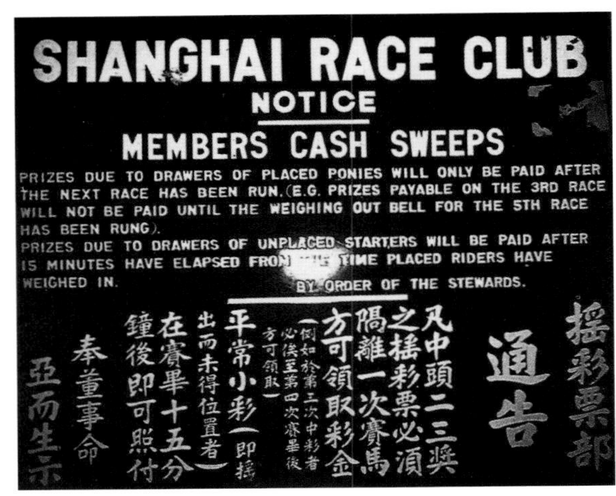

A notice of the Shanghai Race Club.

The race course was an arena for gambling. It generated 150 million yuan from 1920 to 1939.

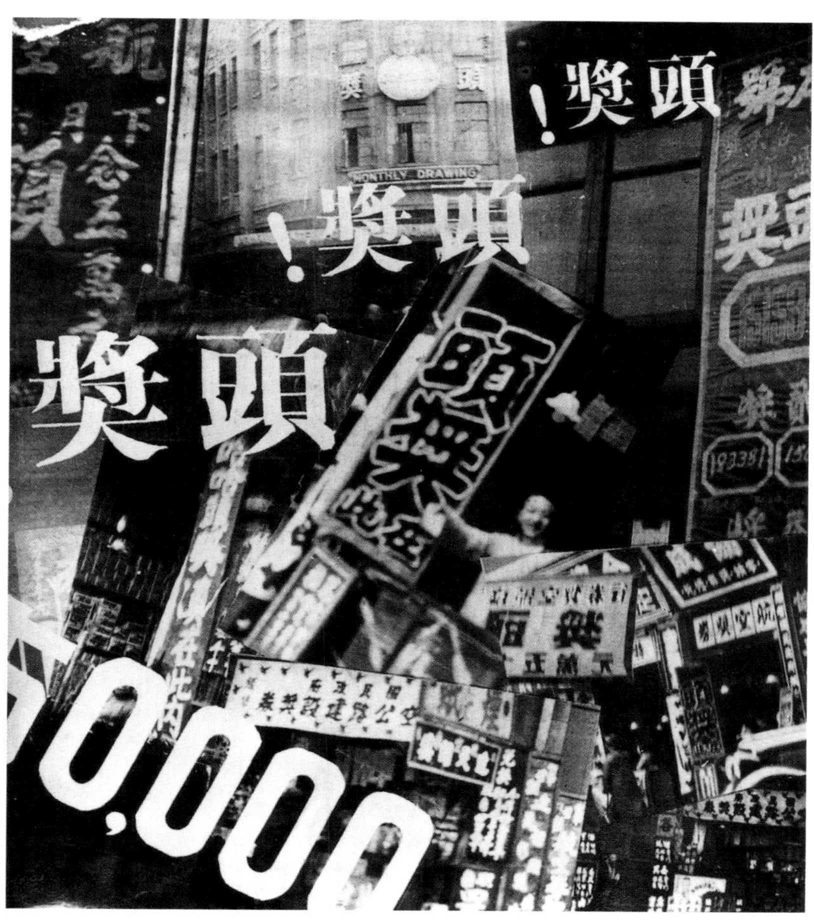

An advertisement for the Shanghai Aeronautical Lottery in the 1930's.

A congee-selling stand in the 1920's.

Peddlers in the International Settlement.

Sellers of Little Stalls

A fortune-teller (1930's).

People with their hands tucked into their sleeves, their shoulders hunched, sizing up pedestrians, must be the sellers in little stands. Holding a fixed though small place, either at the edge of a city gate, a street corner, or entrance to a lane, they hawked their wares but did little business.

Little stalls may seem out of place in a metropolitan city. But this was not true. Local residents with mediocre and low income in Shanghai mostly relied on those little stalls for food and daily necessities. To set up a stall selling congee in front of a restaurant may sound ridiculous, but these did exist and were indeed an incomprehensible street scene. Though such stalls were banned from the areas where there were living quarters of the rich in order to keep the place quiet and clean, the stall owners, however, could find their places to earn a living.

There were also peddlers traveling from street to street. Their hawking has now become legendary and something that is somewhat artistic.

Peddlers crowded the International Settlement in the 1920's.

A tinker

A fortune-teller.

A fortune-teller.

Portrait of Hu Die, Queen of the film world, in 1933.

Plump Women

Ruan Lingyu, who starred in *A Spring Dream in the Capital*, *Goddess*, *A New Woman*, etc., was known in the West as the Chinese Garbo.

Film queens, young women from celebrated families, sociable ladies, dancers, and the modern women of Shanghai in the old days were generally plump, with a serene and fair-complexioned face. The women painted on calendars, be they film stars, a girl of a renowned family, a good wife, or a kind mother were similar in appearance.

As it was a fashion to be plump, everyone wanted to follow the main stream. There must have been slim women at that time, but it is difficult to find one in old photos. Why was this so lopsided in a city like Shanghai? Nobody knows.

So the image of a woman in a particular period of time was fixed. When I close my eyes, plump women with smiles appear in front of me. This is a "collective fantasy" caused by the pictures, which makes us miss some truth that once perhaps existed. Beautiful? Kindhearted? Docile? Healthy? The postures of some women in front of cameras are not reliable at all.

Shanghai policewomen practicing shooting (1936).

Women professionals (1936).

Calendar portraits painted by Hang Zhiying.

Dancers of Shanghai in the 1930's.

Entrance to the Metropolitan Dance Hall.

Four Dancers

Without photography, we would never see these four dancers. Their smiles, joy, and reserved and coquettish manner existed for only a moment. Even the *qi bao* they wore has long since turned to dust.

Let's have a good look at their dress. Two of them wear *qi bao*, and the other two are in frocks. The two in frocks seem to be bold with breasts covered by a thin layer of lace. With their arms folded, the women look reserved and gentle. They must be well educated. The curves from their waists to their feet make one think of their warmth and the sexiness hidden inside.

It would be extremely difficult to find out who they were. If only one of them were still alive, then we might ask for some information, even a little, or at least some remembrances.

Dancing was an occupation as well as a concept. A photo can present a moment of time: four dancers standing side by side, bright and young.

At that moment, they were halfway through their lives. Their futures were unpredictable. Each of them probably had their own plans for the future. The backdrop behind them is not clear. Perhaps it is a picture of a lotus. Where was this photo taken? There is no trace. The color in this photo is fading and the picture may soon disappear.

A calendar portrait painted by Xie Zhiguang.

The ballroom of a dance hall at the corner of Jingansi Road (present-day West Nanjing Road).

1,400 people attended a dance in a dance hall to provide donations for the building of Hongqiao Sanitorium.

Interior of the Metropolitan Dance Hall.

Playing mahjong at the home of a well-off family.

Playing mahjong.

Mahjong

The recreational activities of the people of Shanghai were rich in variety. Local residents were fond of new things yet they stuck to their old games. The same man might drink coffee as well as smoke opium, enjoy a waltz as well as play mahjong.

Import commodities from the West and local tradition were not always contradictory. If it was fun and interesting, it would be accepted lock, stock and barrel by Shanghai residents, as long as they could afford the money and time.

If anyone is going to produce a film about life in 1930's of Shanghai, they would have to first browse in the archives of old photos. All the furniture, costumes, hair-dos, household utensils, decorative objects, and even facial expressions would have to be found in those photos for imitation. The more detailed the photographs, the better. But there is one thing that is impossible to imitate. That is the special facial expressions that were typical of the period. It was not the expression of a gambler or of feigned politeness. It was the expression of "smugness." Rich in meaning, such

Prostitutes were often invited to play mahjong (late Qing dynasty).

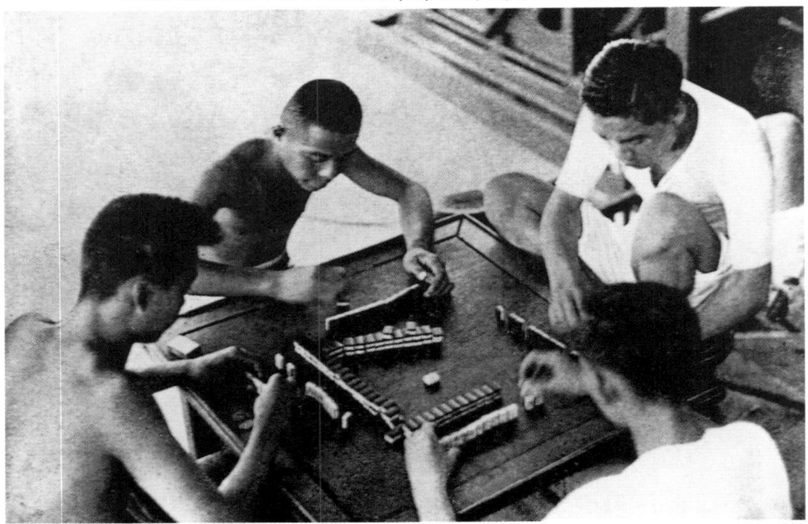

Workers played mahjong after work.

expressions arouse people to ponder over that time.

Mahjong was a household game, so it was most suitable for women. It was a game for four people, so it was also a good social activity for sociable women. It was most suitable for urban married women who could afford the money and time. After a long nap, they might put on some make-up and then get together. While enjoying the eating of baked sesame cakes from the renowned Qiao Jia Shan Bakery, they might gossip about many things such as materials from the Lao Jie Fu Silk and Brocade Store to famous opera stars performing at the Tian Chan Theater, the elopement of Madam Li and Lawyer Dai, the return of a husband from Britain, Garbo and Hu Die? Round after round, the mahjong game would go on and on and soon it would be dusk when the myriad of lights came on.

Playing mahjong, one of recreational activities of urban dwellers.

A parade to celebrate completion of the Clan Hall of Du Yuesheng (1931).

This photo shows Zhai Feng, a member of the Qing Court, passing Nanjing Road (late Qing dynasty).

In memory of four scouts of the Shanghai Chamber of Commerce who laid down their lives in the "January 28 Incident" of resistance during the war against Japan (1935).

A Gathering: Looking on Just for Fun

On the occasion of a party, be it a wedding ceremony, a funeral, a birthday party or a banquet on the weekend, Westerners would be very polite and behave in a most appropriate manner. Disorder and racket would not be permitted. When these got to China, they regarded themselves as civilized people and their way of life became a model to many Chinese.

In this city that just began to be exposed to Western culture, most local residents still stuck to their old ways of life. The fast growth of the population made the hubbub quite chaotic. The funerals, weddings, temple fairs, and festivals were all noisy and seemingly unorganized. When we remember them, we still find them unbearable. It was not an issue of the backwardness of certain rituals. It was because there were too many people and a lack of rules. The original rituals were hard to maintain. There were crowds intermixed with great commotion, crowds looking on just for fun. A local opera in a village, a troupe in a town, country fairs, street crowds gathered for something interesting to see, juggling in the streets, weddings and funerals, people "enjoying performances in theaters of the Great World," and window-shopping were all crowded and filled with commotion, to say nothing of the crowds just looking on.

A film was being shot in the Lianhua Film Studios (1931).

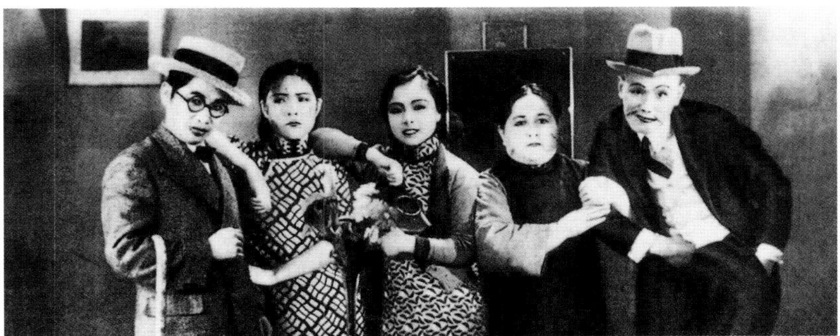

Actors and actresses of *Mr. Wang* made in 1930's. It was about the life of ordinary people.

A spaceship seen in a parade (1937).

Mr. Wang was first published in the form of a serial in a newspaper and was later made into a film by the Tianyi Company.

THE YOKOHAMA SPECIE BANK LIMITED

Chapter 3
Photos Are Traces of the Past

Dutch trade center building (bank) in 1917.

A post office (1908).

Have and Have Not

An empty street, thick foliage, a building in Western style and a cold young woman — these are standing there probably too proud and no one dares go near them. So the photographer had an opportunity to get closer. Behind his camera was his eye. Now it is my eye that is at the position of the photographer's eye. The pictures are of a building, rather far out; mid-noon with a scorching sun; dusk falling and a light can be seen through a window; the enclosure wall makes a bend, a flight of stone steps, a swirling glass door, a roof, serried snow-clad roofs; not a soul in a small lane,; dappled wall; a verandah; tree-lined pavements; dustbin, mailbox, hydrant, and an electrical bell beside a gate; tranquil dawn like that of deep autumn; ground strewn with fallen leaves; a raining season, wet street with reflection of houses on both sides of the street; a sullen afternoon, windows all tightly closed — we have not seen a sign of human beings in those streets, empty streets. I could not help feeling lonely and astonished. This is a city familiar to me but now it is somewhat strange. It seems to be the city that often appears in my dreams. No noise, unbelievably quiet.

A monotonous, straightforward description would leave people unsatisfied. Why are you so interested in such meaningless shots? Because, at this moment, all

Staff and workers of the post office during the late Qing dynasty.

scenes and objects in those shots are things left by human beings.

Leafing over photos one by one until, at last, men have appeared – so many of them, packed in a city. Even the background is blocked by them. The photographer must have been among the crowd, elbowing his way here and there like a naughty boy. But he is lost

The business hall of the Shanghai Post Administrative Bureau.

amidst the crowd. No one pays any attention to him. Ruddy-faced, in high spirits, they push one another and will soon break open the city.

All in all, photos are produced in different places,

On the stands of Shanghai Race Course (1932).

which affects our understanding of them. Feelings determine one's beliefs about the world behind those photos. A moment ago, it was an empty city, quiet and hollow. Now it has become a city of commotion. Hubbub replaces quietness. In the photos of many men, we can see them lining up to buy something, some cheerfully having a picture taken, passengers packed in a bus, onlookers in a street, people at a meeting, old and young viewers of lanterns, performers in a rehearsal hall, visitors in an exhibition hall, kids playing in a lane,

A scene at Tushanwan.

hurrying pedestrians – they pay no attention to their appearance, chaotic, unorganized, unkempt, disorderly. But the general impression is full of vitality. In a city, lively scenes tend to make one excited; empty scenes are thought-provoking. The two different groups of photos serve as an explanation, a witness.

A monument on the Bund.

公共汽車
東站

Westerners enjoyed themselves in their own home garden (1871).

A Western funeral procession (late Qing dynasty).

A steamship appeared in Shanghai.

The Second Hometown

There were all sorts of people living in Shanghai. Many of them took the city as their second home. There were Jewish millionaires, big-shots from Ningbo, Indian policemen, English managers, Guangdong chefs, refugees from Huaibei, French attaché , writers from Sichuan, Japanese performers, and Russians. Residents in old Shanghai, though different in appearance, might consider Shanghai as their second home. Today they live probably in the same place – Heaven. If you look at it in this way, Shanghai to anyone is a second hometown. The scene in any photo is another world, which is separated from us by time. Every time I look at those photos, my imagination either grows stronger or is weakened.

Hardoon (1849-1931), the richest man in the Far East. Hardoon had been a door-keeper for the Sassoon Company. He became rich by trading in real estate. Hardoon Garden was a famous private garden at the time.

The Thousand Flower Pagoda in the Hardoon Garden.

The Wind-listening Pavilion in the Hardoon Garden.

Indian policemen in the foreign concession.

A monument to the dead French soldiers in the Baxianqiao Cemetery.

Emblem of the Shanghai Volunteer Corps.

Officers and Soldiers of the Shanghai Volunteer Corps in 1870.

A little homeless child begged in a street by beating a drum.

Unknown Photographers

A photo without a signature resembles a forsaken boy who is unable to find his mother. He wonders amidst a sea of people, all alone. Gradually he establishes himself before the others. But there are always riddles and there are never any answers to them. For instance, who were the photographers? Why not leave their names?

Photography, in its early days, was not regarded as an original art. It was a simple mechanically operated device. Target an object, a street scene, a man or a get-together, and push the shutter. That's it. It was only a fashionable game, like driving a car, playing with a megaphone, roasting a steak, or wearing a tie. Traces of human life have been handed down by photos. This miracle has been created by machinery and chemistry, not by the one who released the shutter. Therefore, it is not strange to have no signature on those photos.

Still, we are able to guess more or less the occupation and social status of those who took the photos by looking at them. They must be some overseas Chinese, missionaries, reporters or tourists from the West, curi-

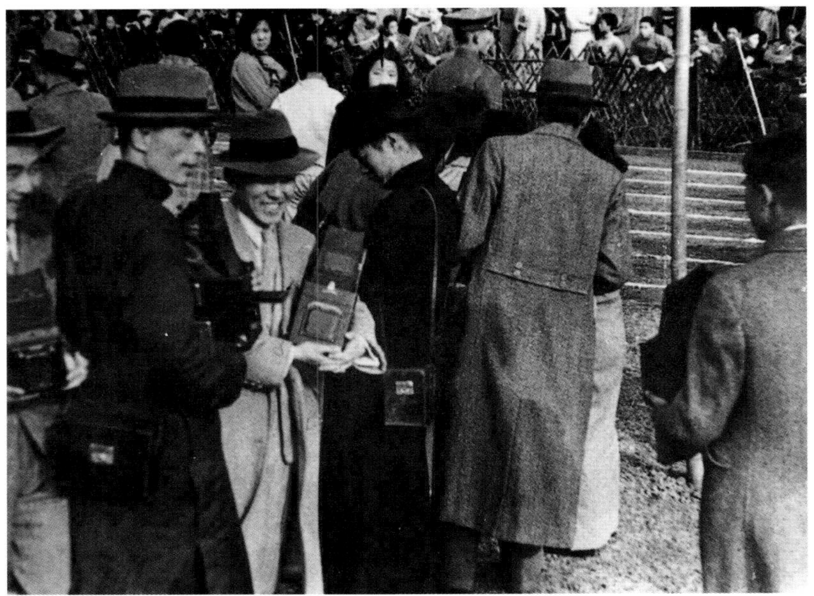

Reporters of the Republic of China.

ous visitors, newspaper reporters, youngsters of well-off families, artists, government functionaries, hosts of a birthday party, the staff of photographic studios, city planning engineers or their assistants.... We can further surmise their purposes for taking those photos: needs for colonialism, secrecy-seeking, collection of news, souvenirs, hunting for novelty, recording of fashions, recording evidence, publicity, sketches, materials for writing, trade secrets, showing off.... One thing is for sure, they are no "works of art."

Just because they are not "works of art," the styles and personalities are irrelevant. Those photos with no signatures are therefore "objective." Their significance lies in the photo itself.

The Huayang Telephone Company.

Many Buildings Are Like This

If you don't look at the caption, you might think this to be a scene from Britain described under the pen of Charles Dickens. When I saunter along a street, I sometimes come across a building that seems familiar to me. When did I pass it before? With whom? Maybe in a film, or perhaps from photo albums preserved by my father. Members of a whole family stand by the building, dressed in similar style. The window shutters, enclosure walls and dome of the building are all pictured. The adults and children, tall or short, are all in clean clothes. The sun is good too. All were included in the photo by the click on a heavy, old fashioned camera. It is difficult to tell who those people were. After all, it was taken dozens of years ago. Only the building exists, but it is becoming aged. There are many buildings like this in Shanghai, numerous indeed.

Building of a foreign company stands by the Yangjing Creek.

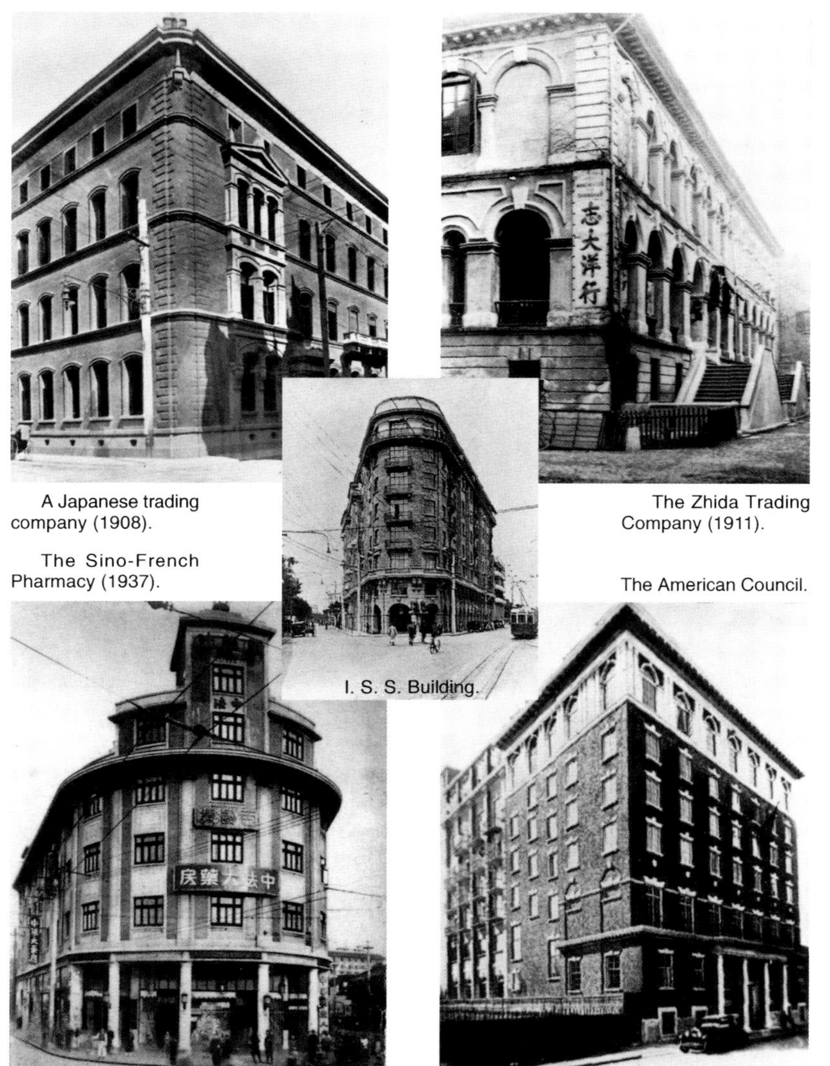

A Japanese trading company (1908).

The Zhida Trading Company (1911).

The Sino-French Pharmacy (1937).

The American Council.

I. S. S. Building.

The Sassoon Mansion, completed in 1928.

The Sassoon Mansion.

Sasson Mansion and A Jazz Troupe Composed of Elders

History has often been excluded from our vistas. This is of course regretful, yet a matter of natural happenings. If you are interested in the modern history of Shanghai, you will not merely have a feeling of enjoyment, like that of tourists, when you stand by the Huangpu River and gaze at the high buildings with neon lights. You will sigh with emotion. Your sigh might start with the Sassoon Mansion. Sassoon was a lame man with a plaque on his car marked 2222, a real estate developer, a greedy money grubber, a cunning philanthropist who donated a large sum of money to Jewish refugees in Shanghai. If you look further back in time, you will find that evil and grandeur appeared hand in hand: opium dealer, seller of textiles from Bombay, chief finance administer of Baghdad. These are all members of the Sassoon Clan. This also reflects the mobile life struggle of the Jews, colonial expansion, an epitome of modern history of Asia and China. Over a span of a century, the Sassoon families have become millionaires in the East: David, Elias, Victor. Three generations of adventure, speculation, far-sightedness and strategies.

Ducheng Hotel.

A Jew with British citizenship named Sassoon set up a trading company in Shanghai in 1845. In 1934, his grandson, Victor Sassoon, built the Sassoon Mansion. The photo shows the eldest son of the third generation of the Sassoon Trading Company.

However, the Shanghai people of today are no longer interested in all this. If you ask young men and women where the Sassoon Mansion is, most likely they have no idea. If you ask where the Peace Hotel is, they will give you an accurate direction. They will probably tell you that there is a very good Jazz Group made of some elderly musicians at this hotel, and there is good coffee too. The atmosphere there is excellent.

History has in this way receded from our horizon.

Now only a Jazz Group remains, reminding coffee drinkers of the past.

Cathay Hotel, located at the junction of Pushi Road and Rue Cardinal Mercier (present-day Changle Road, South Maoming Road), was completed in 1929. It was the highest building in Shanghai at that time.

The orchestra of the Shanghai Municipal Council.

Typical country villas owned by British people.

Flower girls.

Stage Sets

I am fascinated by this picture of a tranquil scene. Two symmetrical English country villas resemble twin sisters standing at the entrance to a street. They remind me of stage sets. Performers are yet to enter the stage, but the curtain has already been drawn. It makes the audience anxious to see what will happen next. A gray sky, a pitched roof and a chimney, a verandah and a flight of steps, and a low fence, all seem so strict, cold, dull, and wealthy, the smugness of the middle class.

This is an old photo of a true place. The building on the right still stands at the junction between Huaihai Road and Huating Road. It is indeed old. Besides, there are more and more pedestrians, customers, people hurrying to take subway trains, awnings, street signs, electric lines, advertisements, dustbins, parked cars, metal railings, billboards.... All together, they have blocked the beautiful house.

Those objects, big or small, which keep increasing in number, have been witnesses of various periods of history: residences of well-off families, the second home of foreigners, a place of revolution which has now become a market.... Those residences must have housed some stories unknown to the public. Unfortunately, they are all scattered. Or perhaps people involved have all lost their memories? Many men of letters try to pry into those stories. Their inspiration comes from hearsay. Not every story is worth writing. A English villa may not necessarily produce a Hardy. What Hardy saw was that hypocrisy killed beauty, but not the "taste".

A cigarette poster.

The former building of the Jardine, Matheson & Company. It was rebuilt in the early 20th century (1917).

GREAT CITY SHANGHAI
THE MOST BUSIEST INTER-
NATIONAL HARBOUR IN ORIENT
CATHAY

The Cathay Cinema, one of the best-known movie houses in Shanghai, on Avenue Joffer (present-day Huaihai Road) opened in 1932.

To live in such a house might make life tasteless. Only the photo makes me spellbound because it has become a drawing of a stage set. People say a stage set is lifeless. Only when performers appear on the stage, does the stage set become meaningful. But it might be just the opposite. There are many people who are insignificant to me. But the houses, soundless stage sets, that they once lived in have left us much for thought.

Inside a Chinese residence.

Inside the luxurious residence of Yu Qiaqing (1867-1945), head of the Shanghai General Chamber of Commerce.

The editorial office of the Wenhui Evening News (1908).

Interiors of Dwellings

The interiors of the dwellings of the poor are rarely seen in these old photos. The walls of a room, furniture, odds and ends, souvenirs, etc. are the best materials to reflect the life standards, people's customs of an era. Perhaps the lack of such pictures is due to technological limitations. It might be too dark inside a poor man's room because of the lack of adequate lighting facilities. Or maybe only well-off families might be able to afford taking photos at home. Anyway, at that time cameras would be too luxurious for commoners. So their lives were excluded from any optical recordings. If we do see those commoners in photos, they usually appear in "public places" such as factories, streets, fairs, etc. The strain of life is written on their faces. Their expressions reveal their uneasiness. They are shabbily dressed. Unfortunately, we have no opportunity to see what their homes would look like and how they whiled away their time at home.

There are a number of photos available that reflect the indoor life of the middle class or above. But they look more or less the same because of the influence of vanity and vogue at the time. Even the backgrounds, objects and life styles are similar: hair-dos, fragrance, wall paper, cupboards, ties, painted eyebrows and mouths, pots and cups, curtains, a megaphone, the verandah leading to a garden....

A calendar portrait painted by Hang Zhiying.

The great revolutionaries Sun Yat-sen (1866-1925), Huang Xing (1874-1916), and others discussing the founding of a provisional government.

An advertisement for the Shanghai Telephone Company.

Interior of a dancing school on Jingansi Road (1933).

The famous Zhangyuan Garden (late Qing dynasty).

Luxurious villa in Shanghai in the early 1920's.

Xieqiao General Chamber (present-day Xieqiao of West Nanjing Road).

Mysterious Villas

If you were to take a walk aimlessly in a street under thick foliage one day, you might suddenly see a villa (or several villas) behind an iron gate or a section of a tumble-down wall. The corner of the wall would probably be covered with moss and the patterns of the iron gate might still remain there. You might guess who was the owner? As time passes, many buildings have collapsed. But this one is still standing. Was it the property of an official, an entrepreneur, or someone who just lived in the building? Words like bankruptcy, deprivation, a change of hands might enter your mind. During different periods of time, who would have benefited, who had to move out. Maybe someone will be able to tell its history. But this is not necessary. You will pass it and leave it behind. You will not bother to find it out.

What will remain in your mind is the word

"mysterious," This is often what your impression of this city will be. There are always stories hidden from us. In albums or in some historical records, one will suddenly recognize something and utter, "So this is the building! It always stands in a certain street, and I often pass it." But all you know or share is its façade, its contour, its foliage. But you will never know about the people who had once lived there. They belong to another world.

A villa built by an English merchant.

The luxurious apartment building of the Yeguang Real Estate Company in the early 20th century.

A view of the Bund in the French Concession as seen from the Bund in the British Concession (1900).

Fuzhou Road in the late Qing dynasty.

Old Streets in Pictures

There are people who rarely go out of their homes but are most interested in the streets depicted in old pictures. Their love for an old map never exhausts them. Their eyes follow along one street after another, and their imaginations become activated. But what is it that is so attractive?

An old street has long since disappeared and the people who once lived in it have mostly gone to Heaven. If you go and visit such a place, what can you see? It reminds me of the stage sets. A drama may remain for a hundred years, but much would be changed in the sets. They may be repaired, and with new things added. They can never be just like the original.

But the drama will not change. Take the name of a street, for instance. It has its former name, other names

Shanghai. Bund in French Concession.

The Bund in the French Concession (late Qing dynasty).

it used in the past, and its name today. Those who rarely go out of their homes will suddenly recognize the street and say, "So it is that street!" After recognition, they might say with a sigh, "Oh, it was not like that at all. It was far better!" or "Oh, it has taken on a new leaf! Time really flies!" The prosperity of the earlier times may have turned into desolation or vice-versa.

An old street is captured in a photo. It is entirely preserved. It may have been demolished, destroyed in a fire or war, rebuilt, and broadened. However, nothing can change the scene of the street in the photo. So a photo is more lasting, except that it can be destroyed

Residential area in Hongqiao (1932).

Avenue Edward VII (present-day East Yan'an Road), built on the site of the Yangjing Creek of the past.

as well.

A man who rarely goes out of his home will find these photos incredible: a view of the French Concession as seen from the British Concession (1900), the Bund within the French Concession (late Ming or early Qing dynasty), Avenue Edward VII (present-day East Yan'an Road) that used to be the Yangjing Ditch, an apartment building at the west end (Hongqiao) of the city (1932), Guangqi Road (1937). The other one seems familiar. That is the Sassoon Mansion and the Bank of

Guangqi Road (1937).

China. But if you look at them a bit longer, you may mistake them for the backdrop for a stage: apathetic, distinctive. But no warm feeling is aroused. One might even feel that those two imposing structures are sham.

The Sassoon Mansion, an architectural structure of the early Modern School, was built in 1928. Next to it was the Bank of China.

A scene of Fumin Road (1920's).

Money lending stores on Jiangxi Road.

Pharmacy and Soy Sauce Shop

Pharmacies and soy sauce shops were mostly like large mansions on the street during the late Qing dynasty. Tall walls written with huge characters in the calligraphic style of Yan Zhenqing served as signboards. They were awe-inspiring. If one looked from a distance, they might appear to be like a frightful yamen, the government office in feudal China.

If you entered a pharmacy, you would be immediately assaulted by a sweet smell. A beam of sunlight would be thrown onto the high counter through the top opening of the little yard. Several men would be standing in the shade ready to serve customers by fetching medicines from various drawers of the large cupboard behind them. Stored in those drawers were "pills, tablets, ointments, and powder from all parts of the country." There were little scales, abacuses, lanterns, urns, each in its own place.

If you dropped into a soy sauce shop, you would smell a fragrance. There displayed would be all sorts of jars and vats. Available were peanut butter, sesame paste, sweet flour paste, shrimp paste, crab paste, bean paste, and pepper paste. Then there would also be all kinds of pickles.

The owners of those soy sauce shops in Shanghai during the late Qing dynasty were mostly from Haiyan in Zhejiang province. Famous pharmacies such as the Hu Qingyu Pharmacy, Cai Tongde Pharmacy and Tong Hanchun Pharmacy were also run by Zhejiang people.

A century ago, the pharmacies and soy sauce shops stood side by side on Nanjing Road. Along this street there were women in robes, rickshaw boys enjoying the sunshine, and vendors at the street corners. What a peaceful street scene. But they would never know the drastic change that would take place in this city with Nanjing Road at its center.

Shops along Zhejiang Road (early 20th century).

A fruit shop on Nanjing Road.

A grocery on Nanjing Road.

A roast duck store.

A taxi company of the 1930's.

Silver Taxi Service

In several books, I found the same photo of taxis taken in 1930's. There are no intruders or other irrelevant objects in this photo. They are standing in a neat row, as if exhibited for a certain purpose. Is this an advertisement of that time? Maybe. The highlight is six light-colored taxis and six cab-drivers in light-colored uniforms who are ready to go. The large numerals 30030 on the wall of the garage, looking like carvings in bas-relief, must be the telephone number. Then there are words in English: Silver Taxi Service, Shanghai Auto Service. All those words, either in English or Chinese, indicate the function of this building. Besides, they give the impression of reliability and elegance. Finally, don't forget to notice the numbers at the top of the wall "1928." It must have been the year when this building was built.

According to records, there were only two imported motor-vehicles in Shanghai in 1901. That year was only a few years after the invention of motor-vehicles abroad. But around 1910, there appeared taxi companies such as Sheng Fu Ji, Hua Sheng Yi, Heng Tai. I am not sure if "Sheng Fu" is a translation of the sound for the word "silver" or the word "service." That being the case, I would say it is a good translation, though there is a great difference in meaning.

Anyway, the translation, which might be inaccurate, did not affect the function of the taxis. What we see in this photo is clear, concise and practical.

A sign for a bus stop (1931).

A double-decker bus.

There is no message behind it. Shanghai people were very practical. What they cared for was the utility of something imported, not giving it a new name.

A 10-horse-power Ford served as a delivery truck for the General Post Office.

A hearse carried by eight people.

A tram (1929).

A new ferry boat.

Fire engines pulled by horses stood in front of the Shenjiawan Fire Station in Wusong Road (1908).

Traffic at the junction of Central Tibet Road and Fuzhou Road.

A public telephone booth in the International Settlement (1930's).

A transparent letter box in the business hall of the Shanghai Post Administrative Bureau.

Public Telephone Booths

Generally speaking, public telephone booths stood at the roadside, lonely and neglected. Pedestrians hurried by or skirted around such a booth, each lost in his or her own thoughts. No one cared much about their existence. Only when one wanted to make a call, would he look for one and push its door open to lift a receiver that had not been used for a long time.

A public telephone booth, which was rarely used, resembled an empty room always waiting in expectation for people. Such booths often appear in films, which may create suspense. It could be a place to arrange for dating, a place from which a voice proposed blackmail, a hope in an emergency. The telephone booth gets one connected with a far away place in a second. It enables a pair of lovers to convey their love for each

Bicycle-riding postmen of the Shanghai Post Office (1920).

other, enables a man to repent, a merchant to do business, a secret agent to pass information. We may converse with one another through using a phone booth.

Let's now have a look at the photo of a public telephone booth by a roadside in a concession in Shanghai during the 1930's. As far as its architecture is concerned, it looks quite unique and clumsy. A man

The building of the Shanghai Post Administrative Bureau (1924).

with a bowler hat is on the point of entering the booth. To its sides are some pedestrians. A conversation is about to begin. The moment is frozen for ever. The man with his arm stretched out has now become a statue in the Street.

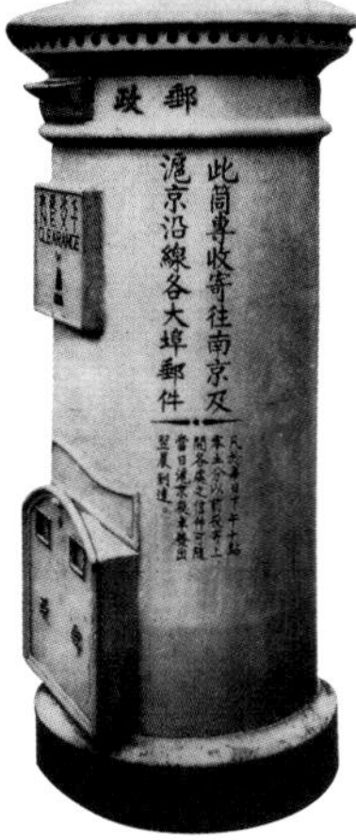

A letter box for a special route in a Shanghai street.

The Garden Bridge spanning where Suzhou Creek and the Huangpu River met (1908).

The Fox Film Company was shooting a film in Nanjing Road.

The residence of Sheng Xuanhuai (located in Central Huaihai Road).

Interior of a room of Sheng Xuanhuai's residence (1920's).

An abacus used by Sheng Xuanhuai, a renowned merchant engaged in foreign trade. Sheng started as a comprador and later ran textile mills, banks, coal mines and a railway. He was appointed Minister of Post Communications by the Qing Court in 1911.

Sheng Xuanhuai's Abacus

This luxurious house seems pompous but without any particular style. The abacus on the desk in the next photo is eye-catching. It indicates the occupation of the owner and his habit. A great merchant, Sheng Xuanhuai, checked all the accounts himself. He was a symbol of cleverness and diligence. He spent his late years in Shanghai. However, he was unable to part with his abacus. Was it his motto, his plaything, or a daily necessity? The furniture in this room is all in Western style except for the abacus.

Sheng died in 1916. This abacus that he used for the best part of a century will probably enter a museum.

The Commercial Press Co. Ltd. (1932).

The office building of the North China Daily (1908).

Dadong Bookstore was located on present-day Fuzhou Road (1920's).

Wangping Street (present-day Central Shandong Road) in the late Qing dynasty.

Industry of Newspapers

A newspaper would collapse immediately if its news and other reports failed to cater to its readers. The reading public of early days was composed of individuals who had different interests yet shared some of the same tastes. Reporters, editors and serial story writers tried hard to cook up stories to satisfy the urban citizens. They had eyes and noses as sharp as hounds in order to catch anything that might be made into news, and to write up things that did not exist. To feed the kaleidoscopic world, they churned up all kinds of writings that came fast and vanished fast. Dozens of years later, these newspapers have become treasures housed in archives and they are most useful to historians.

The launching issue of the Sheng Bao Daily. The Sheng Bao Daily was established in 1872 and stopped publishing in 1949. It was the longest lasting and most influential newspaper in China before it ceased publication.

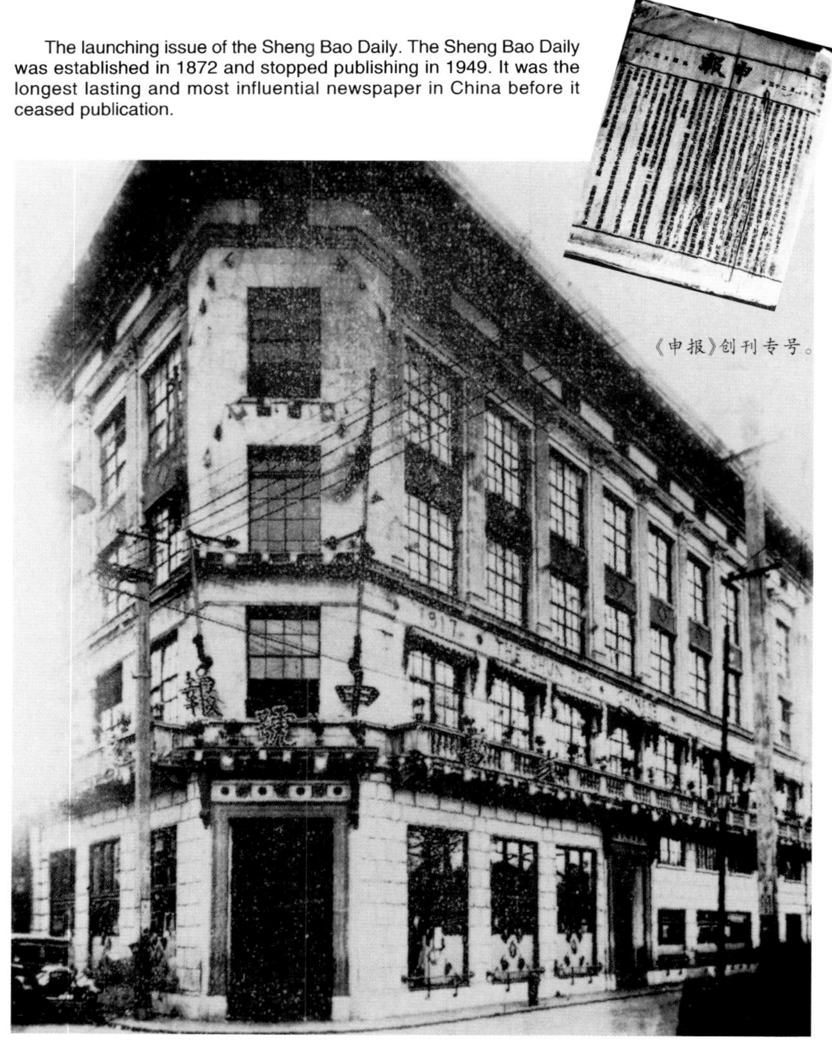

《申报》创刊专号。

The new building of the Sheng Bao Daily.

Newspaper boys got their newspapers from the presses in Wangping Street, a place with many printing presses (1920's).

Newspaper boys.

呢絨嗶嘰
40
VIOLA DANA

Chapter 4

A City with Human Temperature

The Park Hotel of the 1930's.

Sun Sun Company, one of the four leading department stores in Shanghai.

Famous Old Brands

Just imagine, if you were in Nanjing Road a century ago, what you might see there. You would not be able to find the Da Guangming Cinema, nor the Sincere Company. If you walked from east to west, you would probably be amazed that there were so few people. Then you might see the signboards of some stores. The huge, vigorous characters would be written on the two sides of a gate. The same characters would also written on the lintel, or carved on a horizontal board that was hung high on the lintel, or even carved on the stone slates of the façade. The most eye-catching ones would be "Old Fengxiang," a bank, "Shao Wansheng," a grocery, and "Old Jiefu," a silk store. There you would see a few people sauntering in front of these stores. You could not help thinking: These stores, these characters, these people were in harmony with Nanjing Road. Each brick, each tile, each brushstroke, each move of the people were steady,

Fengxiang Bank in the 1920's.

unhurried. They had all the time in the world. But a hundred years later, everything has changed. The buildings, the people and the street of today have undergone tremendous changes. Only the names alone of those stores, though brief, have been preserved as trademarks, a memory, and old brands. The calligraphic characters in vigorous brushstrokes seem out of place in an environment of neon lights, huge glass windows, spic and span stores and escalators.

Interior of the Sincere Company (1925).

Sincere Company (1930's).

Shanghai Wing On Company (present-day junction of Nanjing Road and Zhejiang Road).

The Old Jiefu Satin and Brocade Store, jointly started by the Zu Clan of Fujian, was the oldest store of its kind in Shanghai.

A scene taken after the completion of the Shanxi Road Bridge.

Strangers

A man's ability to deal with matters and people is limited. In a large city like Shanghai, one can feel lost. It is too large, complex and self-contradictory. It is like a sea, so vast and infinite. One has to curb one's ambitious desire to know everything. It is better to keep one's eyes on the things one is capable of handling. Very often, people do not communicate with one another. They are strangers to one another. Their paths may cross in a public place, but they may not belong to the same world.

Look at the photos. They indicate that people may live in the same space and at the same time, but they are at the same time far apart from one to another.

The Lyceum Theatre (present-day Shanghai Art Theatre) was built in 1930.

Lyceum Theater

This beautiful structure sat at the junction of Changle Road and Rue Cardinal Mercier. It has a history of more than 60 years.

Its façade remains the same as it was when first built. Particularly this is so with the three arched windows and balconies. They are the symbol of this structure.

On top of the structure there were large letters spelling out: LYCEUM. They were striking and pompous.

During the day, many people passed unaware of the building's existence. Only in the evening did lovers from all parts of the city come here with tickets. They would then notice the brightly lit letters and the splendid contour of the building.

A drama of a love story was being staged at the Lyceum. The couple in the advertisement seemed to be expecting something. The advertisement was designed

The French Trade Center, built in 1921, was a typical French villa-style structure.

like a painting. There was nothing pompous about it.

I took the photo and went to an art gallery diagonally opposite from the theater and made a comparison. The size of the name was no longer as large. An advertisement indicated that what was scheduled was films and Suzhou ballad singing. Many people passed the entrance gate. Many cars and buses passed by the junction. What was missing was that cast-iron street lamp.

Motion picture was first introduced into Shanghai in 1896. After dozens of years of development, Shanghai won itself the name of "Hollywood in the East." This photo shows a film actress in a studio.

A Large Stage

The mobile life and diversity of people's origins have led to the so-called "alienation of urban dwellers." This caused the collapse of clear-cut periods of time and the boundaries of areas from which dwellers from the same hometown came. This enabled Shanghai to provide opportunities for people to get rich overnight. One might disappear in a sea of people and stage a comeback. One might camouflage his true identification and start from scratch. No one would query his origin. One did not have to stick to one place, nor to be loyal to one social group. He might use several masks and play different roles on different stages.

Shanghai is one of the earliest cradles for drama and films in China. Apart from the local performers, it also attracted a large number of actors and actresses from other parts of the country. In fact, Shanghai itself was a large stage. Its changeable life produced many good performers.

Preparing for a film shooting (1931).

Han Yunzheng and Zhu Fei were in a film (1935).

Churches

A cathedral stood on the southern side of Yangjing Creek (present-day South Sichuan Road).

It was some thirty years ago when I first visited the Xujiahui Catholic Church (Ignatius). I am unable to recall what I saw at that time. All I remember is that it was a fine summer afternoon. The sunlight was dazzling and the front of the church was covered with waist-high weeds. Later on, I looked at some pictures of this church, which supplemented some of the details in my memory.

I have been to Xujiahui many times but each time I was on a buying spree in its business center. Occasionally, when I lifted my head, I saw the two spires of the church behind some high buildings. The church seems so remote to me. It is actually drowned in a sea of buildings.

A church in the city seems more and more like an office building. It functions like a service department. It only provides either regular ceremonial services for its believers or occasionally for someone for an important moment in life. It no longer gives people a fundamental answer. So in Shanghai, it has won its own position in a small way despite all the weal and woe it has experienced. It stands side by side with other structures, but has lost its former central position – belief.

From looking at an album of churches, I have learned something about the history of Catholicism in China, what the missionaries did, the differences in architectural styles, the philanthropic activities, the education

Interior of a cathedral (on present-day Jiujiang Road), designed on the basis of a 13th century Gothic cathedral.

and medical treatment it provided, its cultural infiltration, and its discrimination and attraction. One evening I saw many believers coming out of a church at the junction of Tibet Road and Hankou Road. Their clothes, their expressions were not different from that

A cathedral stands at the junction of Hankou Street and Yunnan Street. It was rebuilt on Central Tibet Street in 1930.

of other people in the streets. I stopped to look at the old church and felt it was amazing that that building had been standing there for over a century. It would be harmonious if it were located in an old university in the United States (from a sheer aesthetic point of view). But it stood in the business center of Shanghai! However, such a sharp contrast might indicate its confidence and ignorance of the secular world.

St. Ignatius Cathedral (present-day Xujiahui Cathedral) was also built in French Gothic style.

Tianshan Theatre was first built in 1925. Renowned Peking opera stars of Beijing and Shanghai, such as Mei Lanfang, Lin Shusen, Ma Lianliang, gave performances here.

Paper-made Archway: An Old Theater

Because of the long years, this old theater in the photo, a place once full of commotion, looks like a paper-made archway. It is shining and must have been painted only recently. Local operas moved from villages to the noisy city and attracted merchants, idle concubines, amateur opera singers, literati, and urban dwellers who had also migrated to the city from the villages. It was years later that those old operas turned into a precious cultural heritage. Only after a local opera or an opera performer died did people begin to realize what a loss had occurred. Protection of culture became a charitable act only when that culture declined and was close to extinction.

Old theaters were usually situated at junctions of streets. It was the best place to gather a crowd. All theaters were decorated in a colorful, complicated and exaggerated manner. They were striking yet vulgar. However, this was most attractive to the public.

Old theaters were built at first of brick and wood. Gradually, concrete replaced the brick and wood. The forms also changed. The upturned roof corners, color-

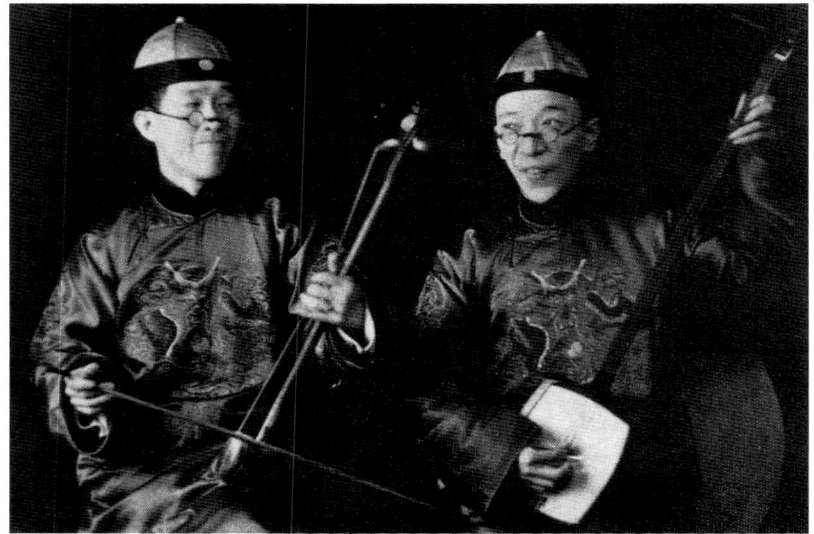

Bao Lele and Jiang Xiaoxiao, the best-known comedians of Shanghai.

ful decorations, plaques written with the names of famous opera stars, and exaggeration were replaced by a style of neatness and simplicity.

Watching a performance in a teahouse.

The First Stage of Dangui, built in 1884 and located in Fuzhou Road, was one of the most popular theatres for Peking opera.

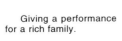

Giving a performance for a rich family.

Building of the Hongkong and Shanghai Banking Corporation.

The building of the Hongkong and Shanghai Banking Corporation in its early days.

A pawn shop in old Shanghai.

Pawnshop

Under a dim light, there was a huge character "Dang" (meaning "pawnshop"), which seemed heavy, ruthless and dull. It did not seem to fit into the Westernized city. However, Shanghai was not a city with only one life pattern. Even today, streets of Xiaodongmen and Nanjing Road are still very different in style. Take the matter of a loan with a mortgage for example. An old-fashioned pawnshop and the Hongkong and Shanghai Banking Corporation belonged to two different worlds in so far as the way money was handled. A bank might make one excited whereas a pawnshop depressed one. A pawnshop was like a yamen, deep and unfathomable.

A bar in a hotel.

A Shanghai café in modern times.

A bar on Avenue Edward VII (present-day East Yan'an Road) in the period from the 1920's to the 1930's.

Coffee Shops on the Map

Who can find the locations of old coffee shops such as the "Sullivan" or the "Sevilla" on the map? It must have been very different from what it is today. But how different? Is there any difference in the smell of a cake or a cup of coffee? The people of the last generation who were fond of coffee must be senile by now. Their teeth must have rotted away and they can only toddle along. And their memories are not reliable at all. It would be too much to ask them to tell us how the coffee tasted, who they met in those coffee shops, what interesting topics they talked about or anything at all that happened on those nights or afternoons.

Those fragmented memories seem reliable. "Sullivan" was strict, like an English gentleman. "Sevilla" was completely different. It reeked of Egyptian tobacco, Vodka, and was full of smoke. People of different colors came and went and spoke all kinds of languages there....

The Nanking Theatre (present-day Shanghai Music Hall) (1936).

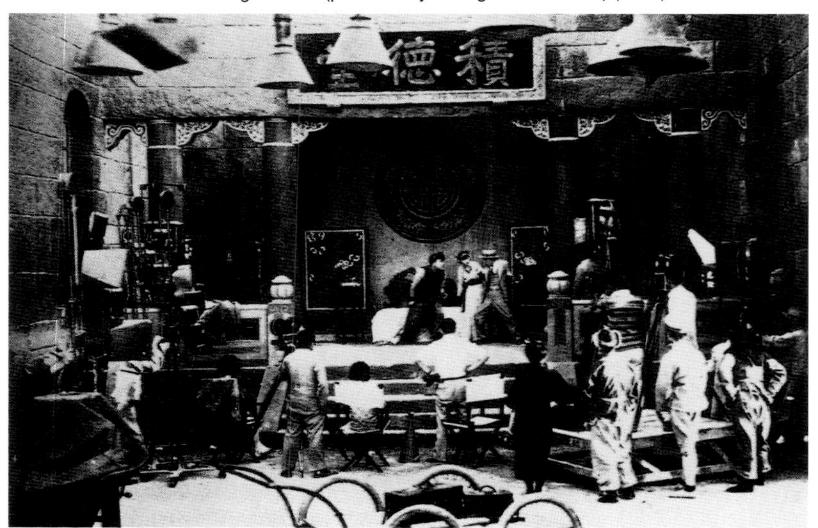

Early days of film shooting in Shanghai.

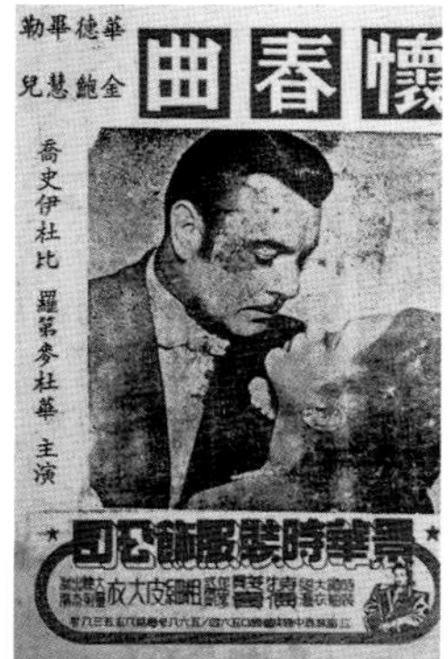

An advertisement of an American film.

Inciting Cinemas

Thinking back, I wonder when Shanghai people began to pursue things in vogue. Did film have anything to do with it? Films made people realize that their life was dull and isolated and they began to feel unsatisfied with their situation. Daydreaming, ambition, inflated desire, knowledge, news, shows of an exotic life made them dissatisfied. Once those demons were let out of cinemas, they greatly affected the life pattern of the city. Those with money and the desire to seek for things modern, and those who drifted along with life, regarded what they saw in films as their fanciful world, a new land. The films not only served as entertainment but also as an example to follow.

There were many reasons why Shanghai people had such a strong interest in a new and strange life. But it is reasonable to say that films played an important role. When one entered a cinema, they entered a dark "dreamy city." It provided a chance for them to avoid reality which was often not happy. So the cinema served as a vehicle to incite dissatisfaction.

The Huashang Cloth Exchange.

Telephones in the Shanghai Stock Exchange.

The trading floor of the Shanghai Stock Exchange.

To Suit the Contemporary Times

The stock exchange has now come into our lives. This affects the orientation of comments on this phenomenon. In fact, there is no fresh point of view. The secret of historical comments lies with the value that must suit the times.... The conclusion is often laughable as time changes. So clever historians just shut their mouths and engage themselves in copying some anecdotes and legends, recording others' reminiscences and leaving the comments to posterity.... No need! Anything that suits contemporary times is right. Fear of being out of date? Your profession is bound to be out of date sooner or later, unless you have given it up entirely.

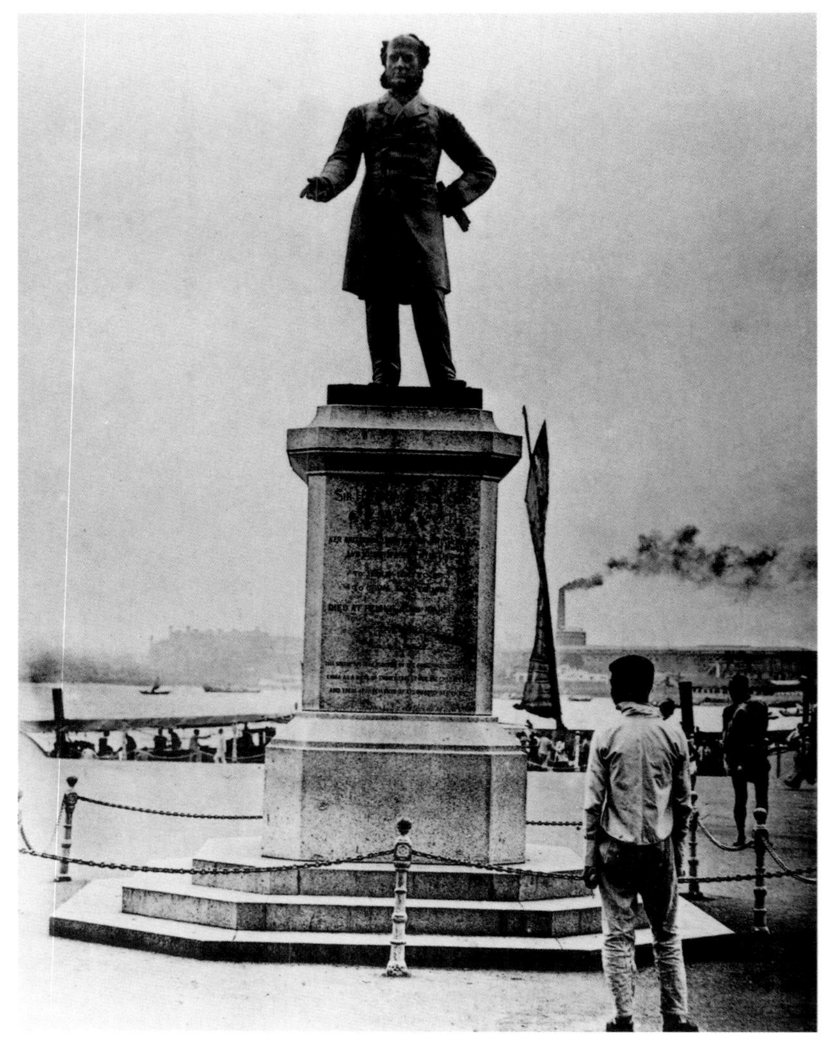

The statue of the British consul in Shanghai in 1863.

A French airplane (early 20th century).

Out-of-Date Annotations

The annotation of historical records is used mainly to fill the blank space between photos. This is because of the need for layout in a publication, for the purpose of some rhythmic or visual changes. The main theme is the photo. It is the verse of a song. As soon as you look at it, you have a clear picture. Annotation is supplementary. It is the opening bars to an accompaniment. A photo shows you something real and is convincing. It keeps to the original scene (the scene when the photo was taken) whereas annotation keeps changing from time to time. This means that annotation easily becomes out of date.

The German Consulate.

The British Consulate.

The French Consulate.

The Russian Consulate.

The American and German Consulates on the northern bank of the Wusong River.

The Japanese Consulate.

The British and American troops who were stationed in Shanghai retreated before the breakout of the war between the United States and Japan in 1941.

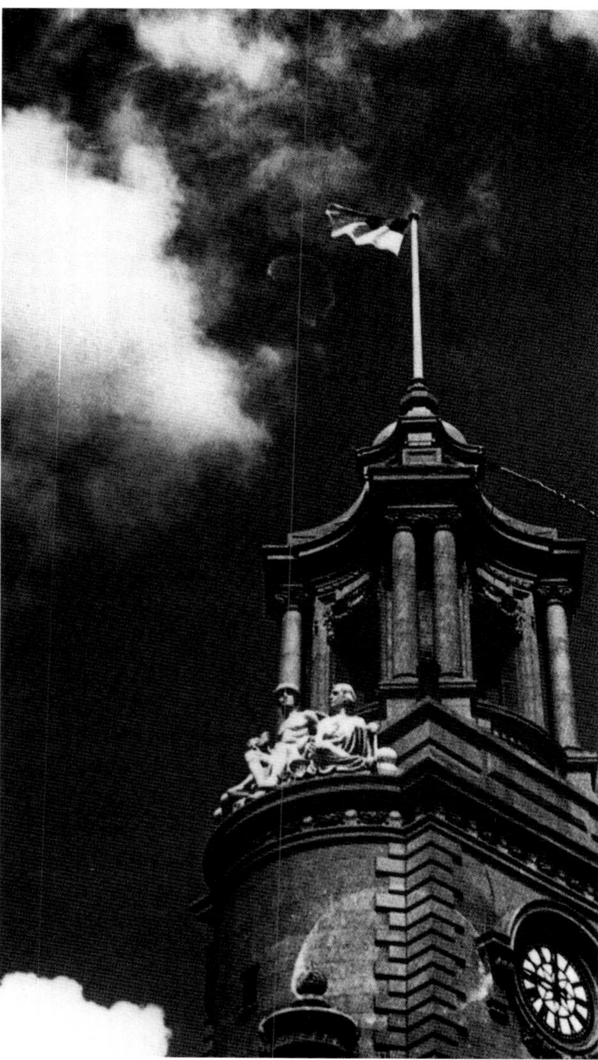

Statues on top of the building of the Shanghai Post Administrative Bureau (1914).

Erecting an electric street lamp (1937).

Inconsistency

Letters that appear beside a photo can be misleading. This is nothing strange. It would be impossible to look at the photo without reading the letters.

Location, architectural style, owner of the house, time when the famous brand was created, obvious fashions, all have records to be looked into. Inconsistency lies with "views": praise, humiliation, indignation, contempt, admiration.... This is the subjective view of writers of today. When looking back in history, readers have to stand by the writer. Therefore, they have fallen into "a trap of view" set by others.

In compiling an historical story with photos, distortion becomes inevitable. A photo has many functions. It is as if it had several doors. You may enter

Shanghai Museum (1936).

and be led in different directions. Inconsistency is such a door. If you happen to choose such an entrance, you will be muddle-headedly led to another street. So a photo may be used as an illustrative diagram for a classroom.

Letters are part of a photo. As long as they stay where they are, they should be honest and true.Abduction needs charms. It also needs a reader's self-

Hankou Road and the Customs House during the late Qing dynasty.

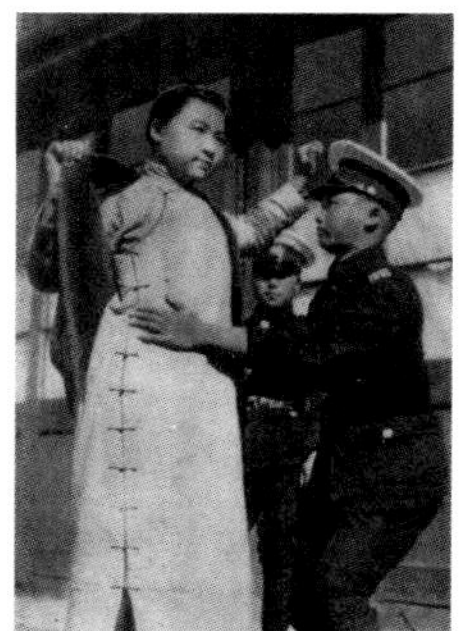
A policewoman on duty.

suggestion: willingness to elope. To elope is a dangerous impulse. It is a result of a long term agony. So when a chance arises, a reader may just follow blindly. Luckily, such elopement is completed in a reader's own room. When he wakes up and returns to reality, he would smile and said that it is all nonsense.

Having a picture taken in a photo studio (early 20th century).

The entrance to Fudan University.

The entrance to Jiaotong University.

Progress, Fashion

The first art school in China – the Shanghai Art School – was founded in 1912.

Large cities were hotbeds of radical thinking. Only in large cities did the trends of thought and fashion keep changing. Customs and new needs combined into one, showing themselves in daily life, and then spreading to other parts of the country. Shanghai was an international city with a changing life. So anything coming from the countryside would be sooner or later doubted. Things Western in Shanghai enjoyed a high esteem. Their position was much higher than those things that were handed down by ancestors. The so-called "worship and have blind faith in things foreign" is a negative phrase. It contains the meaning of curiosity, seeking for new things, and longing for an exotic life. In a metropolitan city everything changes rapidly, including beliefs, hobbies, feelings, etc.

Professor Cheng Dexu of Fudan University and his family (1930's).

Nanyang College had a Normal School (high school) when it was first established in 1896. Later on it set up its Outer School and Central School. The photo shows the building school.

The Peace Monument to the European War was erected on the Bund near East Yan'an Street on 16 February 1924. It was pulled down by the Japanese army after the fall of Shanghai.

Demolition

The Goddess of Peace on the Bund, the North Railway Station, stands of the Horse Racecourse, the French consulate and many other structures have all been demolished. The sites where they once stood are nowhere to be seen. They have been replaced either by a gray sky or some other towering buildings.

Old photos are able to fill the gap. Demolition means ruthless eradication of structures overnight. Buildings, particularly old buildings, serve as landmarks in our memory. Once they are out of sight, no matter for what reason, our memories are soon unable to find their way home. Luckily, we have photos. However, photos often make us grieve.

An old-fashioned towboat.

The Sichuan Road Bridge and the Post Administrative Bureau on the bank of Suzhou Creek.

Flooded Streets

I once had a dream that is unforgettable. The city was flooded and all its buildings were standing in water. It became an island. I could see no one. Everyone else was asleep and was having the same dream. They also saw the city flooded. The sky was low and gray, reflecting the shimmering water on the ground....

What I saw in the dream was vague. When I recalled this later, the reliability of the dream was doubtful.

I would never expect that a photo taken a century ago would be similar to what I saw in that dream. Besides, the scene in the photo is much clearer. This photo is from an archive and it leaves no room for doubt. The photo shows a flooded street, tightly closed windows and doors of buildings on both sides of this street. The signboards of the stores remain, facing an empty street.

Refugees in Chongming county of Shanghai.

The photo shows the earliest "Boundary Road" (present-day Central Henan Road) during a flood in the 1880's.

Today in history, a photo, a far-fetched dream, a record in script, urban geography and textual research on meteorological history have formed complicated relationship. How shall we choose? Photos may perplex people with different experiences. It is a dumb show with the simplest explanations. An expert on the local history may tell us the evolvement of a street for a century. What about a painter? What he is interested in not the flow of history, but a still scene. Surely, for photos, if it is leafed over, it is leafed over. What's really interesting is yet to come.

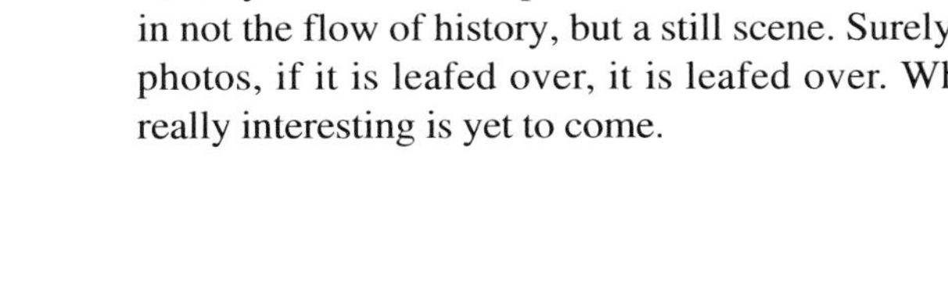

Refugees in Shanghai lived in dilapidated and small shacks.

Chapter 5
Through the Door of Impression

The interior of the Richard Hotel. The hotel was pulled down in 1907.

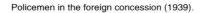

Policemen in the foreign concession (1939).

The funeral procession for Lu Xun (1936).

Photography, Revolution and Documents

Thinking back to past events: invasion by foreign powers, internal insurrections, deteriorating villages, infiltration of Western culture, the Westernization Movement, the New Reform, going abroad to study, running of enterprises, the rise of education, foreign powers and revolution, trends of thought and political parties ... each has left its trace on Shanghai.

The introduction of photography into China and its application has developed as history progressed. Photography also went through periods of revolution, resistance, pledges and fighting. In this respect, photography is a witness, not an art. Photos serve as evidence of important past events. Today, they have already become keepsakes, portraits of late renowned figures, documentation in archives, historical records, which are locked up in drawers as items in different categories and for the purpose of historical research.

Hu Die was known as "Queen of Asian Films." Starring in silent films, talking films, and films dubbed in Mandarin or Cantonese, she became the best-known actress in China.

This image of Hu Die was used for advertisements of Lux soap.

A Repeatedly Used Photo

A repeatedly used photo may not be a photo of historic significance. Maybe it is just used out of convenience. You don't have to browse in your treasure chests, you don't have to attach a caption, nor do you have to explain the origin. It is like a portrait of a film star that can be seen everywhere in Streets, in store windows, in advertisements, and on the covers of magazines. Who cares about its origin? Reproductions of the photo exist everywhere and anyone can take it as his own.

Nostalgia for the past has been in vogue for quite a number of years. Nostalgia for the past has even become a thing of the past. So nostalgia for the past itself has become something for remembrance. However, the basic theme of nostalgia always recurs. This is why photos are used repeatedly. An old song, whose author is anonymous, has been sung generation after generation. The same melody, the same mood: sadness, to bid farewell, to miss someone, nostalgia for a hometown. The tune may sound different to different people. Yet there exists unified "collective fantasy."

The basis for the continuation of such a collective fantasy is the song's repeated broadcasting, singing, quoting and publishing. The recurrence has become embedded in our neural reaction system and connects to our fixed concepts. So when I see an old photo, I

The new building of the Shanghai Council (1917).

think of an era, an atmosphere, a sound and slow pace.

Repeatedly used photos play an important role in our visual life. Together with other relics, they have become a kind of montage element that chases and exceeds time. It has been melted into an incredible and real daily life. Old photos entice us to think of the glory of past generations, unaware of the fear of their death. Therefore, repeated use of old photos is on a par with building up a railing around us.

In July 1876, the Wusong Railway (from Shanghai to Jiangwan), built by foreigners and the first railway in Shanghai, started operation. The photo shows people standing along the railway to watch the train. Later on, the Qing government bought this railway and demolished it, and then rebuilt it in 1897. It was completed and put in use on 1 September the following year.

Local residents worried that the electrical poles might jeopardize the Feng Shui.

Public Resistance

According to historical records, in the latter half of the 19th century, the network of water transportation not only covered the interior of the country but also reached Shanghai. The railway cut through the fields, disturbed the peace of the ancestral graves, and easily caused fear and anger among the people. Electrical poles, too, met with some hostility from the local residents. This was because they feared that those electrical poles would harm their Feng Shui. They were therefore frequently sabotaged.

Such scenes cause reflection, a sense of nationalism, sorrow and pain, grief over the folly, and sympathy. Photography has captured these worries, which cause you to hold your breath as you gaze at a scene. Would those people ever know that scenes of their struggle for a better existence would be one day included in an elaborately published album and be read by literati of later generations? Literati, who are keen on taste, stop their eyes for a brief moment at such photos and then turn the pages quickly.

As soon as one entered the "Joy Gate," he would come to the roof garden of the Sincere Company.

The roof garden of the Sincere Company.

"Another Page of Life Has Been Turned"

There is a message behind each photo. The roof garden of the Sincere Company in this picture was a good place for entertainment. A party was going on but it would soon pass. A message was demonstrated through a negative: joy, following the trend, was like a dream. Outside the picture stood Nanjing Road which was open to anyone, its store windows, brightly lit neon lights, and stores with dazzling lamps. If one looked down over the railing of the roof garden, one would never forget that night....

No wonder an artist said, "Another page of life has been turned."

Editor's Note

Changes a city has undergone are an important part of the history of the development of a civilization. In publishing this series of books, we have been guided by one consideration, i.e., to give readers a brief history of some well-known Chinese cities by looking at some old sepia photos taken there and reading some remembrances with regard to those cities.

Not like conventional publications, each book of this series contains a large number of old photos selected to form a pictorial commentary on the text. This provides a good possibility for readers to learn about Chinese urban history, cultural evolution in urban society in a new perspective. It also enables readers to re-experience historical "vicissitudes" of those cities and relish feelings of urban folks of China in the modern times.

To better illustrate those cities, we have commissioned renowned writers who have not only lived in their respective cities for a long time but also have been known for their strong local writing style. Either in presenting a panoramic view of a city or depicting fate of men in street, their writings are always so natural yet full of feelings.

This series of books have been published originally in Chinese by Jiangsu Fine Art Publishing House. The English edition has been published jointly by the Foreign Languages Press and Jiangsu Fine Art Publishing House.

Foreign Languages Press
Oct. 2000 Beijing

图书在版编目(CIP)数据

老上海:已逝的时光/吴亮著;王明杰译. —北京:外文出版社,2001.5
(老城市系列)
ISBN 7-119-02845-6
Ⅰ.老… Ⅱ.①吴… ②王… Ⅲ.散文-作品集-中国-当代-英文Ⅳ.I267
中国版本图书馆 CIP 数据核字(2001)第 18623 号

中文原版

选题策划 叶兆言 何兆兴 顾华明 速 加
主　　编 朱成梁
副 主 编 顾华明 孙永鑫 张 伟
著　　文 吴 亮
图片供稿 中国第二历史档案馆 上海图书馆
装帧设计 顾华明
责任编辑 顾华明

英文版

策划编辑 兰佩瑾
翻　　译 王明杰
英文编辑 卓柯达
责任编辑 王文通

老上海·已逝的时光

外文出版社出版
(中国北京百万庄大街 24 号)
邮政编码 100037
外文出版社网址:http://www.flp.com.cn
外文出版社电子信箱:info@flp.com.cn
sales@flp.com.cn
利丰雅高制作(深圳)有限公司印刷
2001 年(大 32 开)第 1 版
2001 年第 1 版第 1 次印刷
(英文)
ISBN 7-119-02845-6/J·1565(外)
08000(精)

OLD CITY

APITOL
CAPITOL